Table of Contents

Introduction	3
Public Awareness of Local Schools	6
Perceived Importance of Education/Schools	9
Goals of Education and the Role of the Public Schools	11
The Public's Appraisal of Public Schools	12
Most Important Problems Facing Public Schools	17
Ways to Improve Public School Education	18
Factors Affecting School Quality	20
Acceptance of Education Innovations	21
Finances	23
Federal Government and the Schools	28
Private and Parochial Schools	30
Curriculum	31
Computers	40
Who Should Choose Instructional Materials/Books?	41
Schoolwork and Homework	41
Extracurricular Activities	43
Testing	43
School Attendance	46
The Uninterested Student	49
The Handicapped Student	51
The Special Student	51
Academic Self-Evaluation by High School Juniors and Seniors	52
Discipline	53
Drugs, Alcohol, and Smoking	57
Crime	58
Student Rights	59
Integration and Racial Issues	60

Table of Contents

Parental/Citizen Involvement	62
Teachers and Teaching	67
Principals and Administrators	73
School Boards	74
College	76
Youth Unemployment Jobs	77
Adult Education	78
Preschool	78
National Commission on Excellence in Education	79
Miscellaneous	79
Looking Ahead	81
1984 Gallup Poll of the Public's Attitudes Toward the Public Schools	83

Acknowledgments

Dr. George Gallup and his staff prepared the document, *Topical Report: Annual Surveys of the Public's Attitudes Toward the Public Schools, 1969-1983*, on which this volume is based. This categorization of the nearly 400 questions asked of the general public in the United States over that 15-year period, and the summaries of answers, were generously forwarded to us by Alec Gallup in the spring of 1984. The questions include those reported in the annual Gallup Polls of the Public's Attitudes Toward the Public Schools published in the *Phi Delta Kappan* plus a few others asked in other polls conducted by the Gallup Organization.

Phi Delta Kappa owes a great debt of gratitude to the late Dr. George Gallup and his staff for compiling this data and releasing it for publication. I also would like to recognize the scrupulous work of David Ruetschlin, staff associate in the Phi Delta Kappa Division of Special Publications, for checking all of the figures in this compilation against the original reports.

Introduction

This volume summarizes findings of the annual Gallup Polls of the Public's Attitudes Toward the Public Schools of the U.S. for a 15-year period, 1969 through 1983. In the final pages it also reports in full the 1984 poll, as published in the September 1984 issue of the *Phi Delta Kappan*.

This summary reveals certain striking trends in public opinion about the public schools. Most ominous for the well-being of America, perhaps, are trends reflected in the answers to just two questions: 1) How do you rate your local schools (on an A, B, C, D, F scale)? and 2) Would you like to see a child of yours take up teaching in the public schools as a career?

Between 1974, when the question was first asked, and 1983, the percentage of people rating their local schools A or B (i.e., excellent or good) dropped from 48% to 31%. There was a corresponding increase in the lower ratings: from 11% rating their local schools D or F in 1974 to 20% in 1983. Even allowing for some sampling error, these figures represent a negative change of opinion by 25 to 30 million people (there are about 170 million voting-age adults in the U.S.). It is a significant change indeed.

In response to the second question, in 1969 about 75% of parents interviewed said that they would like to see one of their children teach in a public school. In 1983 only 45% said that they would like one of their children to be a public school teacher.

Do such answers mean that U.S. schools are less effective now than they were a decade ago? That teaching is less attractive as a career than it was in 1969? The answer to the first question is, "Not necessarily." The answer to the second is, "Probably yes." A rational judgment on the first has to be based on dozens of facts and factors not directly related to public opinion. Explaining and analyzing these factors is beyond the scope of this volume. But I would feel remiss if I did not mention some of the more obvious factors. So let us take a closer look at the drop in school approval rates. Gallup has noted that parents with children in school always rate their local schools higher than do people who have no children in school. He believed that this difference reflects at least two interlocking facts: 1) Parents know a good deal more about the schools and can make more accurate assessments than nonparents. They are heavily influenced by firsthand knowledge, whereas the opinions of nonparents derive more often from the media, which tend to report only negative or sensational events. 2) There are far fewer respondents with children in school today than there were in 1974. In that year 39% of Gallup's respondents had children in public schools and 55% did not. In 1983 the first figure had dropped to 27% while the second rose to 68%. (In 1974, 8% of the respondents had children in nonpublic schools; in 1983, 6% did.) These factors alone could account for the 10-year downtrend in ratings, and they are unrelated to school quality.*

As for the 30% drop in the number of parents who would like to see their children take up teaching, probing by Gallup interviewers revealed that the prime factor was the surplus of teachers in the Seventies and early Eighties. Parents didn't want their children to prepare for nonexistent jobs. Other significant factors included the well-publicized economic disadvantages of teaching, the growing prevalence of teacher burnout, and increasingly attractive opportunities for women in other fields. (There was a time, of course, when teaching — which is still predominantly "women's work" at the elementary level — represented one of the few respectable career opportunities open to young women.) In 1969, the year that Gallup education polls were initiated, nearly one-quarter of all students enrolled in U.S. colleges planned to

---

*Psychological imponderables are at work here, too. How does the proprietary interest of parents in their local schools affect ratings? Does resistance to being taxed to educate other people's children affect ratings by nonparents and, if so, how?

become teachers. By 1980 that fraction had dropped to one-twelfth. No wonder teacher shortages began to reappear very recently.

Clearly, raw data from the poll cannot be properly assessed without drawing on related information. Readers of this book should remember that. Also, it is important to view the figures in this volume in historical context. Note that the period since 1969 has been especially difficult for many people connected with education. It was a time of broken dreams. For example, the promise of federal intervention to solve some of education's most intractable problems was never fully realized. Lyndon Johnson, who had hoped to be a great "education president," was dragged down by Vietnam. The Elementary and Secondary Education Act of 1965, perhaps his greatest education legacy, did not presage the massive infusion of federal funds that would be required to achieve educational equality among the states; and this is one of America's continuing scandals. Other federal initiatives of noble intent failed or were crippled for a variety of reasons — conceptual inadequacy, underfunding, bureaucratic inertia, etc.

The collective bargaining movement in education that swept the country in the early and mid-Sixties was only marginally successful in producing economic benefits, better working conditions, and enhanced status for teachers. So long as there was a teacher shortage, bargaining at the district level did help, particularly in the large cities. But when the post-World War II baby boom had receded, there were surplus teachers and surplus classrooms. During the 14 years between 1970 and 1984, the number of school-age children dropped by 6.2 million — enough to fill 12,400 elementary schools at 500 pupils each. (New York State alone lost 700,000 children in that age group.) Not for another 10 years will we gain back perhaps 75% of the school population lost in the last 14 years.

The population factor combined negatively with "stagflation" — sluggish growth in the GNP, monetary inflation, and unemployment. Together, these factors meant that teachers actually lost purchasing power in the Seventies.

And then there was Watergate. Social scientists have noted that a pervasive loss of faith in most of our social institutions accompanied the Watergate revelations of mendacity in government. Education did not escape, although loss of public confidence in the schools was less marked than loss of faith in several other public institutions. George Gallup said, in reporting the 1974 poll, "The public schools represent one of the two or three American institutions which have held the respect and confidence of a majority of citizens in a period of widespread cynicism and disillusionment."

As the above discussion suggests, it is easy for the public to misjudge the schools. It is just as easy for educators to misread the meaning of opinion polls. The best antidote in both cases is a fund of related information. That information must be supplied and disseminated, insofar as possible, by leaders of the profession. In the words of one of the poll's originators, Edward Brainard, the function and purpose of the public education poll is "to obtain information for public school educators — information that will help them better serve their students and their communities." The "information" Brainard refers to consists largely of images in the minds of people. If these images are distorted and inaccurate — and obviously they often are — it only means that the education profession faces another daunting task: education of the adult public about the schools. As I noted in a *Phi Delta Kappan* critique of the first 15 years of the poll, "Every poll has made clear the need for a constant flow of information to the public from the schools, using every available medium. This flow is particularly necessary today."* The other side of the coin is that there needs to be a generous flow of information in the other direction as well.

This information flow grew notably in the 1983-84 academic year (after publication of the fifteenth education poll). Over the past year, for example, the findings of a number of national studies of education have been reported and debated in the media. For the first time since the late Fifties, the problems of education have become a major national issue. Reforms of many kinds have been considered. As a result, most of the 50 state legislatures have taken action to improve schools, and they should continue to do so through the Eighties.

I doubt if anyone would contend that schools suddenly became dramatically better in 1983-84. Yet the 1984 Gallup poll reveals a dramatic 35% increase in public approval of local public schools in that one year. The percentage of people giving their schools an A or a B (excellent or good) rose from 31% in 1983 to 42% in 1984, the highest approval rating since 1976. George Gallup, who wrote the analysis of 1984 poll findings only a week before his death, speculated that one important reason for this increase in approval was the fact that, as a result of the national debate and its local application, people knew more than ever about their schools and came to recognize their strengths. People also knew that improvements were being made or

---

*See "The Gallup Education Survey: Impressions of a Poll Watcher," *Phi Delta Kappan*, September 1983, pp. 26-32.

were under consideration. Gallup's speculation is supported by the fact that the "don't know" category of respondents to the ratings question fell from 17% in 1983 to only 8% in 1984.

Most Americans are deeply committed to the belief that education is the most important service rendered by government. They continue to feel, according to the poll, that public education contributes more to national strength than either industrial might or military power. They consider education the key to personal success. Thus the heavy critical attention being paid to education today may be a blessing in disguise. Education leaders, as represented by the membership of Phi Delta Kappa, can use the basic positive feelings of the American public about the importance of education as an anchor for reform that will produce better education for all.

* * *

The items in this summary have been arranged topically so that the user can identify and follow trends more readily. Certain questions have been asked repeatedly, although only one (What are the problems of your local schools?) has been asked in every poll. The year in which a question was asked is listed after the question, and related questions are grouped together. Also, throughout this compilation "DK" has been used to indicate "don't know," "no opinion," or "no answer," because the three categories appear to have been used rather indiscriminately in the original reports.

The complete Gallup Polls of Public Attitudes Toward Education are available from Phi Delta Kappa. The first 10 polls are included in the volume, *A Decade of Gallup Polls of Attitudes Toward Education 1969-1978* (price: $5.50, PDK members $4.50). Reprints of each of the polls published in the *Phi Delta Kappan* from 1979 on are also available (price: $7.50 for minimum order of 25). Order from Phi Delta Kappa, Box 789, Bloomington, IN 47402. Demographic breakdowns for the items in this summary are available from the Gallup Organization.

The Gallup/PDK polls will continue to provide some of the information about public opinion that educators need. The Phi Delta Kappa Board of Directors remains committed to financial support of the polls, and membership response to their publication has been very gratifying to those of us who have been involved in designing the questions and analyzing the results.

Stanley Elam
Gallup/PDK Poll Coordinator
1 August 1984

Public Awareness of Local Schools

Level of Awareness

How much do you know about the local schools — quite a lot, some, or very little? (1969, 1983)

	1969 %	1983 %
Quite a lot	18	22
Some	40	42
Very little	42	29
Nothing	-	7

Would you like to know *more* about the public schools in this community?

	1969 %	1970 %	1974 %
Yes	65	54	54
No	35	44	38

Names of Local Officials

Do you happen to know the name of the principal of the high school attended by the children in your neighborhood? ... the president of the local school board? ... the principal of the elementary school? ... the superintendent of schools? (1969)

	Yes %
Principal of high school	40
Principal of elementary school	47
President of school board	26
Superintendent	56

Facts About Local Situation

Do you think there is a shortage of classroom space in this community? (1969)

	%
Yes	56
No	29
DK	15

What is your guess as to the cost per child per year in the public schools of your community? (1969)

	%
Gave a dollar figure	43
DK	57

Are there many high school dropouts in this community? (1969)

	%
Quite a few	26
Almost none	41
Other	3
DK	30

What percentage of the high school graduates from your high school go on to college, do you think? (1969)

	%
Gave an actual percentage	67
DK	33

Sources of Information

What are the sources of information you use to judge the quality of schools in your community — that is, where do you get your information about the schools? (1973, 1983)

	Sources of Information	
	1973	1983
	%	%
Newspapers	38	42
Students	43	36
Parents of students	33	29
Other adults	23	27
School board/faculty	33	24
Radio and/or television	20	19
Personal experience	-	8
PTA	3	-
Other	12	4
Undesignated	4	7

What is your *best* source of information about the local public schools? (1969, 1979)

	1969	1979
	%	%
Local newspapers	38	37
Radio and TV	16	21
School publications/newsletters	8	7
Word of mouth/personal involvement	40	70
DK	6	8

Exposure to Education News in Local Media

During the last month, have you read any articles in the newspapers about local schools . . . heard anything on radio . . . seen anything on TV? (1969)

	Yes
	%
Read newspaper article	60
Heard on radio	36
Saw on TV	35

During the last year, have you received any newsletter, pamphlet, or any other material telling what the local schools are doing . . . read any book that deals with education? (1969)

	Yes
	%
Received written material	35
Read book	16

What is the name of the book(s)? (1969) (Asked of those who said they had read a book.)

	%
1 title given	4
2 titles given	2
3 titles given	*
4-6 titles given	1
No titles given	10
	17

*less than 1%

Since September, which of the following, if any, have you yourself done? (1983)

	National Totals %	No Children In School %	Public School Parents %	Nonpublic School Parents %
Received any newsletter, pamphlet, or any other material telling what the local public schools are doing	32	22	58	38
Attended a local public school athletic event	25	18	42	28
Attended a school play or concert in any local public school	24	16	42	36
Met with any teachers or administrators in the local public school about your own child	21	4	62	44
Attended a PTA meeting	14	4	36	46
Attended any meeting dealing with the local public school situation	10	7	18	13
Attended a school board meeting	8	4	16	24
Written any letter to the school board, newspaper, or any other organization about the local school situation	4	3	6	5
None of the above	43	56	14	22
DK	4	4	2	6

Local Media Treatment

Do you think the news media (newspapers, TV, and radio) give a fair and accurate picture of the public schools in this community, or not? (1977)

	%
Yes, fair	42
No	36
DK	22

In your opinion, how could the media (newspapers, TV, and radio) improve their reporting of education in the local schools? (1977)

The answers elicited by this question often referred to the paucity of news about the schools reported in many communities. But the most frequent response dwelt on the need for more positive news — interesting things the schools are doing to achieve their educational goals.

Many specific suggestions were offered which the media might well consider. Among these were:

"Reporters should be sent into the schoolrooms to see what goes on there. They should put themselves in the teacher's place, and in the student's place."

"It would be interesting to find out about all the different courses that are offered."

"Reporters should talk to students, explore their problems."

"Why don't they [the media] tell us about the standing of the local schools — how well they do in comparison with the private schools, and with other schools in nearby cities."

"I should like to know more about the changes that are being introduced and why. There should be more background information about education and about new programs."

"Outstanding students should be written up and praised the way top athletes are."

"An interesting series could be built around the idea of a typical day at school with a typical seventh-grader, ninth-grader, etc. I can remember what went on in my day. I wonder if it is the same now."

"I hear a lot about the gadgets now used in the schools and in the classrooms to teach different subjects such as foreign language and I would like to know more about them."

"The media report on the school budget, but they never tell, in detail, just where the tax dollars are spent."

"In the magazines I read about 'open' classrooms, 'team teaching,' and such things, and I wonder if our local schools go in for these new ideas."

Perceived Importance of Education/Schools

Relative to Military, Industry

In determining America's strength in the future — say, 25 years from now — how important do you feel each of the following factors will be — very important, fairly important, not too important, or not at all important? (1982)

	Very Important %	Fairly Important %	Not too Important %	Not at all Important %	DK %
1. Developing the best educational system in the world	84	13	1	*	2
2. Developing the most efficient industrial production system in the world	66	26	3	1	4
3. Building the strongest military force in the world	47	37	11	2	3

*Less than one-half of 1%.

Degree Expressed

How important are schools to one's future success — extremely important, fairly important, not too important? (1973, 1980, 1982)

	1973 %	1980 %	1982 %
Extremely important	76	82	80
Fairly important	19	15	18
Not too important	4	2	1
DK	1	1	1

Desired Federal Spending Priorities

If and when more federal money from Washington is available, which one of the areas on this card do you think should be given first consideration when these funds are distributed? And which one of these areas do you think should be given second consideration? And which one of these areas do you think should be given third consideration? (1975, 1982)

1975 Results	First Choice %	Second Choice %	Third Choice %	Combined Choices %
Health care	18	19	16	53
Public school education	16	15	17	48
Law enforcement	11	14	16	41
Welfare and aid to poor	14	11	7	32
Public housing	10	9	7	26
Pollution/conservation	8	8	8	24
Mass transit	6	7	6	19
Military defense	6	5	5	16
Agricultural aid	4	4	7	15
Highway improvement	4	4	5	13
Foreign aid	1	1	1	3
DK	2	3	5	10

1982 Results	First Choice %	Second Choice %	Third Choice %	Combined Choices %
Public school education	21	17	17	55
Health care	19	19	15	53
Welfare and aid to poor	16	15	11	42
Military defense	14	9	10	33
Law enforcement	8	11	13	32
Public housing	8	9	10	27
Pollution/conservation	5	7	6	18
Agricultural aid	3	4	6	13
Mass transit	2	3	4	9
Highway improvement	1	3	3	7
Foreign aid	1	1	1	3
DK	2	2	4	8

Goals of Education and the Role of the Public Schools

People have different reasons why they want their children to get an education. What are the chief reasons that come to mind? (1972)

	%
To get better jobs	44
To get along better with people at all levels of society	43
To make more money — achieve financial success	38
To attain self-satisfaction	21
To stimulate their minds	15
Miscellaneous reasons	11

I am going to read off some of the areas to which the public high schools devote attention in educating students. As I read off these areas, one at a time, would you tell me whether you feel the high schools in your community devote too much attention, not enough attention, or about the right amount of attention to that area? (1981)

	Too Much %	Not Enough %	Right Amount %	DK %
Developing students' moral and ethical character	2	62	21	15
Teaching students how to think	2	59	25	14
Preparing students who do not go to college for a job or career after graduation	2	56	29	13
Preparing students to become informed citizens prepared to vote at 18	2	55	28	15
Preparing students for college	3	43	39	15
Developing students' appreciation of art, music, and other cultural interests	7	37	41	15

Of course all of the qualities listed on this card are important in the overall development of a child. But which *one* do you regard as the *most* important? (1976)

	%
Learning to think for oneself	26
Ability to get along with others	23
Willingness to accept responsibility	21
High moral standards	13
Eagerness to learn	11
Desire to excel	4
DK	2

Asked of High School Juniors and Seniors

What are the overall educational goals of the school you attend? (1974)

	%
To prepare students for college	43
To prepare students for jobs	25
To graduate students and get them out of school	10

What do you feel are the most important things *you* are getting out of school? (1974)

The most frequent answers were "making friends" and "learning to get along with people." These reasons were cited even more often than "gaining a general education" or "preparing for a job after high school." Fourth in frequency of mentions was "preparation for college."

Very few students mentioned goals usually cited by educators: "personal development," "acquiring a sense of values," "widening one's outlook," "becoming more mature." Some students said they had developed a greater sense of responsibility, more self-reliance, and that they had learned to cope better with people and problems; but very few juniors and seniors said that the most important thing they were getting out of school was the development of their individual capabilities.

The Public's Appraisal of Public Schools

Confidence in Institutions

How much confidence do you, yourself, have in these American institutions to serve the public's needs — a great deal of confidence, a fair amount, or very little? (1980)

	Great Deal %	Fair Amount %	Very Little %	None (Volunteered) %	DK %
The church	42	40	15	2	1
The public schools	28	46	20	3	3
The courts	19	45	28	5	3
Local government	19	51	23	4	3
State government	17	52	24	4	3
National government	14	47	31	5	3
Labor unions	17	38	30	9	6
Big business	13	42	36	5	4

What Children Like About Their Schools

What is the main thing that *your eldest* child likes about the school he/she attends? (1982)

	Public School Parents %	Nonpublic School Parents %
Teachers	17	18
Friends	16	14
Sports	13	11
Enjoys learning	13	21
Social program	11	3
Using the library	7	6
Curriculum	6	4
Math	6	1
Art	4	5
Band/choir	4	—
Science class	4	4
Feeling of accomplishment	4	6
Industrial arts	2	—
Miscellaneous	9	12
DK	9	14
Doesn't like school	5	6

What Parents Like About Schools Their Children Attend

And what is the main thing that *you* like about it [the school he/she attends]? (1982)

	Public School Parents %	Nonpublic School Parents %
Quality of education	13	25
Teachers' interest	11	14
Curriculum	11	8
Children are learning	10	11
Qualified teachers	10	5
Faculty are nice	7	3
Location	7	5
Parents kept informed	4	7
Discipline	4	20
Teacher/child relationship	3	6
Students are motivated	3	4
Morals/values taught	1	10
Extracurricular activities	3	2
Emphasis on the basics	1	1
Classroom size	1	2
Miscellaneous	3	4
DK	10	8

Letter Grades Given (Overall)

Students are often given the grades A, B, C, D, and FAIL to denote the quality of their work. Suppose the public schools, themselves, in this community were graded in the same way. What grade would you give: the public schools *here* ... the public schools *nationally*. (1974-83) (National ratings were begun in 1981)

	1974 Local %	1975 Local %	1976 Local %	1977 Local %	1978 Local %	1979 Local %	1980 Local %	1981 Local %	1981 National %	1982 Local %	1982 National %	1983 Local %	1983 National %
A	18	13	13	11	9	8	10	9	2	8	2	6	2
B	30	30	29	26	27	26	25	27	18	29	20	25	17
C	21	28	28	28	30	30	29	34	43	33	44	32	38
D	6	9	10	11	11	11	12	13	15	14	15	13	16
FAIL	5	7	6	5	8	7	6	7	6	5	4	7	6
DK	20	13	14	19	15	18	18	10	16	11	15	17	21

Grades Given Public Schools in Specific Areas

Students are often given the grades A, B, C, D, and FAIL to denote the quality of their work. Suppose the public schools, themselves, in this community were graded in the same way. What grade would you give: the *elementary schools* here/the *high schools* here ... the high schools for preparing students to get a *job/for college* ... the *teachers/principals* and *administrators/parents*. (1981)

	Local Elementary %	Local High School %	Prepare for Job %	Prepare for College %	Principals & Administrators %	Teachers %	Parents %
A	13	7	6	9	10	11	5
B	33	25	20	25	26	28	24
C	27	31	29	29	28	31	36
D	7	15	18	13	12	9	16
FAIL	5	9	12	9	9	6	11
DK	15	13	15	15	15	15	8

Using the A, B, D, C, and FAIL scale again, please grade the job you feel the public schools here are doing in providing education in each of the following areas. (1981) (Asked of parents only)

	A %	B %	C %	D %	FAIL %	DK %
Reading	16	32	27	11	5	9
Writing	12	34	27	12	6	9
Mathematics	13	34	29	10	4	10
Science	11	33	33	7	3	13
Social studies	11	32	32	8	3	14
Music	17	32	22	9	3	17
Physical education	21	41	20	4	2	12
Art	12	30	28	9	2	19
Vocational or job training	8	27	25	15	6	19

Using the A, B, C, D, and FAIL scale again, please grade the public schools in this community for each of the following. (1983)

	A %	B %	C %	D %	FAIL %	DK %
The physical plants and facilities	30	35	21	5	2	7
The curriculum, that is, the subjects offered	24	37	25	4	3	7
The handling of extracurricular activities — sports, theater, etc.	20	33	26	8	4	9
Books and instructional materials	19	33	32	6	2	8
Quality of teaching	13	35	29	12	4	7
Education students get	14	32	29	15	4	6
The way schools are administered	11	28	29	17	8	7
Preparing students for college	12	26	27	17	4	14
The way discipline is handled	11	21	22	20	19	7
Preparing for jobs those students not planning to go to college	7	19	29	20	9	16
Behavior of students	5	19	27	19	22	8

Satisfaction with Present School

Would you like to send your child to a different public school? (1979)

	Yes %	No %	DK %
Parents whose eldest child is 12 years and under	12	78	10
Parents whose eldest child is 13 years and over	11	86	3

If you could send a child of yours to *any* school in this area, to what school would you send him? (1974)

	%
Replied	68
No reply	18
No other school in area	14

Attitudes Becoming More/Less Favorable

In recent years has your overall attitude toward the public schools in your community become more favorable or less favorable? (1973)

	%
More favorable	32
Less favorable	36
No change	23
DK	9

As you look on your own elementary and high school education, is it your impression that children today get a better or worse education than you did? (1973, 1979)

	1973 %	1979 %
School better today	61	41
Worse	20	42
No difference	11	9
DK	8	8

Most Important Problems Facing Public Schools

What do you think are the biggest problems with which the public schools in this community must deal? (1969-1983)

Percentages Citing Each Problem

Problems Cited	1969	1970	1971	1972	1973	1974	1975	1976	1977	1978	1979	1980	1981	1982	1983
Lack of discipline	26	18	14	23	22	23	23	22	26	25	24	26	23	27	25
Use of drugs	—	11	12	4	10	13	9	11	7	13	13	14	15	20	18
Poor curriculum/poor standards/concern about standards/quality	4	6	3	5	7	3	5	14	10	12	11	11	14	11	14
Lack of proper financial support	14	17	23	19	16	13	14	14	12	13	12	10	12	22	13
Integration/busing (combined)	13	17	21	18	18	16	15	15	13	13	9	10	11	6	5
Overcrowding/large schools	—	—	—	10	9	6	10	5	5	5	4	7	5	4	3
Difficulty in getting good teachers	17	12	—	—	13	11	11	11	11	9	10	6	11	10	8
Parents' lack of interest	7	3	4	6	4	6	2	5	5	4	3	6	5	5	6
Teachers' lack of interest	—	—	5	—	—	—	—	5	3	3	6	4	7	8
Pupils' lack of interest/truancy	3	—	2	—	3	2	3	3	3	4	4	5	4	5	5
Crime/vandalism	—	—	2	—	—	—	4	2	2	4	4	4	3	3	1
Mismanagement of funds/programs	—	—	—	—	—	—	—	—	4	3	2	3	3	3	2
Drinking/alcoholism	—	—	—	—	—	—	—	—	1	2	2	2	2	3	3
Problems with administration	—	1	3	—	—	—	—	—	3	2	1	2	3	2	1
Lack of proper facilities	22	11	13	5	4	3	3	2	2	2	2	2	2	2	1
Communication problems	—	—	—	—	1	—	—	1	1	2	2	2	1	1	1
School board policies	—	2	1	—	4	4	1	3	1	1	2	1	1	1	—
Government interference	—	—	—	—	—	—	—	—	—	—	2	1	1	1	1
Teachers' strikes	—	—	—	—	—	—	—	—	—	—	1	1	1	1	1
Parents' involvement in school activities	—	—	—	—	—	—	—	—	—	1	1	1	1	—	1
Too many schools/declining enrollment	—	—	—	—	—	—	—	—	1	1	1	1	1	2	—
Transportation	5	2	—	—	—	—	—	—	2	1	1	1	—	1	—
Non-English-speaking students	—	—	—	—	—	—	—	—	—	—	—	1	1	1	1
There are no problems	4	5	4	2	4	3	5	3	4	4	3	3	3	1	1
Miscellaneous	8	3	6	9	4	4	12	8	5	6	5	2	5	2	2
Lack of respect for teachers/other students	—	—	2	—	—	—	—	—	—	—	—	—	4	2	3
Lack of needed teachers	—	—	—	—	—	—	—	—	—	—	—	—	—	2	1
Moral standards	—	—	—	—	—	—	—	—	—	—	—	—	1	2	4
Fighting	—	—	—	—	—	—	—	—	—	—	—	—	—	1	1
DK	13	18	12	12	13	17	10	12	16	12	16	17	12	11	16

Ways to Improve Public School Education

Ways to Improve (unaided)

In your opinion, what are the main things a school has to do before it can earn an 'A'? (1979)

	%
1. Improve the quality of teachers	23
2. Increase discipline	20
3. Set higher standards	17
4. Give students more individual attention	16
5. Put more emphasis on the basics — the 3 R's	12
6. Better management and direction of schools	7
7. Establish closer relations with parents	6

What, if anything, do you think the public schools in this community should be doing that they are not doing now? (1978)

In order of times mentioned
1. More strict discipline
2. Better teachers
3. Back to basics
4. More parental involvement
5. Higher scholastic standards
6. More education about health hazards
7. More emphasis on careers

Ways to Improve (aided)

Which of these ways do you think would do most to *improve* the quality of public school education overall? (1976)

	%
Devote more attention to teaching of basic skills	51
Enforce stricter discipline	50
Meet individual needs of students	42
Improve parent/school relations	41
Emphasize moral development	39
Emphasize career education and development of salable skills	38
Provide opportunities for teachers to keep up to date regarding new methods	29
Raise academic standards	27
Raise teachers' salaries	14
Increase amount of homework	14
Build new buildings	9
Lower age for compulsory attendance	5
None	1
DK	4

What suggestions would you make to get parents, the community, and the school to work together to improve education in the local public schools? (1979)

Survey respondents had many suggestions, which can be summarized as follows:

1. *Better communication.* The local community cannot be expected to take a keen interest in the schools if people know little about them. The media should carry much more school news, especially news about the achievements of students and the schools, the means being taken to deal with school problems, and new developments in education. Media research has shown that there is far greater interest in schools and in education than most journalists think. At the same time, the schools should not rely solely on the major media. Newsletters are important to convey information that the media cannot be expected to report.

2. *More conferences.* Many of those included in the survey recommend that more conferences about the progress and problems of students be held with parents — both father and mother. Special monthly parent meetings and workshops are also suggested as a way to bring teachers, administrators, and parents together. Survey respondents also recommend courses for parents and special lectures. PTA meetings, some suggest, could be more useful to parents if school problems and educational developments were given more attention.

3. *Invite volunteers.* Some respondents suggest that, if more members of the community could serve in a volunteer capacity in the classrooms and elsewhere in the school, they would further better community understanding of the problems faced by the schools. In addition, their involvement in school operations would increase their own interest in educational improvement at the local level.

4. *Plan special occasions.* Interest in the schools and in education could be improved, some suggest, by inviting members of the community — both those who have children in the schools and those who do not — to attend meetings, lectures, and social events in the school buildings. As noted in another section of this survey report, only one person in three across the nation attended a lecture, meeting, or social occasion in a school building during the last year. In 1969, when the same question was asked, a slightly higher proportion said thay had attended a lecture, meeting, or social occasion in a school building.

Here are a number of things which may have a good effect on the education students receive in the public schools of this community. Will you choose four (from a list of 14 suggestions) which you think are particulary important. (1980)

	%
Well-educated teachers and principals	50
Emphasis on basics such as reading, writing, and computation	49
Teachers and principals personally interested in progress of students	44
Good parent/teacher relationships	40
Careful check on student progress and effort	32
An orderly but not rigid atmosphere	27
Useful materials and adequate supplies	25
Small classes	25
Special classes for handicapped students	24
High goals and expectations on part of students	19
Wide variety of vocational courses	18
Advanced classes for the gifted	12
Extracurricular activities	6
Successful athletic teams	4
DK	6

Factors Affecting School Quality

School Size

Do you think high schools today are getting too large or aren't they large enough? (1973)

	%
Getting too large	57
Not large enough	13
Just right	15
DK	15

Class Size

In some school districts, the typical class has as many as 35 students; in other districts, only 20. In regard to the achievement or progress of students, do you think small classes make a great deal of difference, little difference, or no difference at all? (1973)

	%
Great deal of difference	79
Little difference	11
No difference	6
DK	4

City Size

In general, do you think that students today get a better education in schools that are located in small communities or in schools located in big cities? (1977)

	%
Small communities	68
Big cities	11
Makes no difference	12
DK	9

Additional Money

In some school districts, about $600 is spent per child per school year; some school districts spend more than $1,200. Do you think this additional expenditure of money makes a great deal of difference in the achievement or progress of students — or little difference? (1973)

	%
Great deal of difference	39
Little difference	38
None	10
DK	13

Acceptance of Education Innovations

Readiness for Change

Do you feel that the local public schools are not interested enough in trying new ways and methods or are they too ready to try new ideas? (1970, 1974)

	1970 %	1974 %
Not interested enough	20	24
Too ready to try new ideas	21	20
Just about right	32	32
DK	27	24

In the schools in your community, do you think too many educational changes are being tried, or not enough? (1971)

	%
Too many	22
Not enough	24
About right	32
DK	22

Open Schools

Do you happen to know what is meant by the "open school" idea or concept? (1975)

	%
Knew	27
Didn't know	60
Weren't sure	13

In your own words, how would you describe an "open" school? (1975)

Most of the 27% who claimed to understand the concept proved that they did. A negligible few said it meant "open to all."

How do you feel about "open" schools? Do you approve or disapprove of them? (1975)

	%
Approve	13
Disapprove	10
DK	4

Other Kinds of Schools

For students who are not interested in, or are bored with, the usual kind of education, it has been proposed that new kinds of local schools be established. They usually place more responsibility upon the student for what he learns and how he learns it. Some use the community as their laboratory and do not use the usual kind of classrooms. Do you think this is a good idea or a poor idea? (1973)

	%
Good idea	62
Poor idea	26
DK	12

In some U.S. cities parents of school children are being given the choice of sending their children to a special public school that has strict discipline, including a dress code, and that puts emphasis on the three R's. If you lived in one of these cities, and had children of school age, would you send them to such a school or not? (1975)

	%
Yes	57
No	33
DK	10

Ungraded Schools

Should a student be able to progress through the school system at his own speed and without regard to the usual grade levels? This would mean that he might study seventh-grade math but only fifth-grade English. Would you favor or oppose such a plan in the local schools? (1972, 1975, 1980)

	1972 %	1975 %	1980 %
Favor	71	64	62
Oppose	22	28	30
DK	7	8	8

Should high school courses be arranged to make it possible for some students to finish one year of college work while they are still in high school, so that these students can graduate from college in three years instead of four? (1977)

	%
Yes	63
No	31
DK	6

Performance Contracts

In some public schools, educational companies are given contracts to put in new methods to teach the children in elementary schools certain basic skills, such as how to read. These are called 'performance contracts.' If the children don't reach a certain level of achievement, the company doesn't get paid for those children who fail to reach the standard. Would you like to have such contracts made here, in this community, if the overall school costs remain about the same? (1971)

	%
Yes	49
No	28
DK	23

Finances

Awareness

Do you happen to know what it costs per child, per school year, in the local public schools? How much? (1979)*

Named a figure:	%
Under $700	17
$700 - $1,299	40
$1,300 - $1,899	18
$1,900 - $2,499	10
$2,500 and over	15

*The National Center for Education Statistics estimated the cost per student for the 1979-80 school year at $2,469.

It costs taxpayers about $2 an hour for each student for each class he or she attends — or about $10 for each school day. Are these figures higher, lower, or about the same as what you had thought? (1980)

	%
Higher	29
Lower	19
Same	34
DK	18

Financial Sources

There has been much discussion in the nation about the best way to finance the public schools. Do you happen to know where *most* of the money comes from to finance schools in this community? (1978)*

	%
Property taxes (local)	49
Federal sources	11
State sources	16
DK	24

*In 1978, according to Gallup, in the nation as a whole, 48% of revenues to finance the public schools came from local sources, 44% from the state, and 8% from the federal government.

Are you, yourself, satisfied or dissatisfied with this way of raising the money? (1978)

Those who named:	Satisfied %	Dissatisfied %	DK %
Property taxes	43	52	5
Federal sources	68	21	11
State sources	68	20	12

Do you happen to know whether the schools in your school district receive any money from the federal government (the government in Washington)? (1975)

	%
Yes	50
No	6
DK	44

What part of the school budget in your district do you think this federal money represents — a small part, a fairly sizable part, or a very large part of the budget? (1975) (Asked of those who said that the schools in their school district receive money from the federal government.)

	%
Small	17
Sizable	18
Large	6
DK	9

Attitudes Toward Spending, Forms of Taxation, Etc.

Do you think money is spent foolishly by the school authorities or the local school board? (1969)

	%
Yes	26
No	65
DK	9

Suppose the local public schools said they needed much more money. As you feel at this time, would you vote to raise taxes for this purpose, or would you vote against raising taxes for this purpose? (1969-1983)

	1969 %	1970 %	1971 %	1972 %	1981 %	1983 %
Would vote for	45	37	40	36	30	39
Would vote against	49	56	52	56	60	52
DK	6	7	8	8	10	9

Would you be willing to pay more taxes to raise the standards of education in the United States? (1983) (Followed questions on National Commission on Excellence. See page 79.)

	%
Yes	58
No	33
DK	9

It has been suggested that state taxes be increased for everyone in order to let the state government pay a greater share of school expense and to reduce local property taxes. Would you favor an increase in state taxes so that real estate taxes could be lowered on local property? (1970-1972)

	1970 %	1971 %	1972 %
Favor	54	46	55
Oppose	34	37	34
DK	12	17	11

It has been suggested that state government through increased taxes pay more of the cost of local school expenses. Would you favor or oppose an increase in state taxes for this purpose? (1973)

	%
Favor	40
Oppose	50
DK	10

It has been suggested that a new kind of national sales tax, sometimes called a value-added tax, should be adopted to help reduce local property taxes that now support public schools. Do you favor or oppose such a tax? (1972)

	%
Favor	35
Oppose	51
DK	14

Did you happen to vote in the last school bond election? (1969)

	%
Yes	41
No	49
DK	10

Can you recall how you voted? Did you vote for or against the bond? (1969) (Asked only of those who answered "Yes" to the question above)

	%
For	26
Against	10
Can't recall	5

At present some public school districts spend less than others per child in school. Would you favor or oppose a constitutional amendment to reduce these differences? (1974)

	%
Favor	66
Oppose	22
DK	12

Would you approve or disapprove of a law in this state that would put a top limit on the amount of money which could be included in the local public schools' annual budget? (1979)

	%
Approve	33
Disapprove	42
DK	21
Already have such a law	4

When federal agencies appropriate money for educational programs, they usually require the schools that receive this money to spend it as these agencies direct. Should, or should not, this be changed to permit local school authorities to decide how the money is to be spent? (1977)

	%
Should	62
Should not	29
DK	9

Reducing Expenses

School enrollments in many parts of the nation have declined because of a lower birthrate. If this were to happen here, would you suggest that school expenditures be reduced accordingly? (1976)

	%
Yes	55
No	35
DK	10

Suppose your local school board were "forced" to cut some things from school costs because there is not enough money. I am going to read you a list of many ways that have been suggested for reducing school costs. Will you tell me, in the case of each one, whether your opinion is favorable or unfavorable? (1971, 1976, 1982) (Sixteen proposed means of cost cutting offered in 1971; only eight in 1976 and nine in 1982)

	1971 Favorable %	1971 Unfavorable %	DK %
Cancel any subjects that do not have the minimum number of students registered	52	35	13
Have the school run on a 12-month basis with 3 months of vacation for students, 1 month for teachers	47	38	15
Make parents responsible for getting children to and from school	39	51	10
Charge rent for all textbooks instead of providing them free	34	56	10
Cut out kindergarten	19	69	12
Reduce janitorial and maintenance services	15	72	13
Keep present textbooks and library books although it may mean using outdated material	20	68	12
Reduce the amount of supplies and materials teachers use in classrooms	26	58	16

	Favorable 1971 %	Favorable 1976 %	Favorable 1982 %	Unfavorable 1971 %	Unfavorable 1976 %	Unfavorable 1982 %	No Opinion 1971 %	No Opinion 1976 %	No Opinion 1982 %
Reduce the number of administrative personnel*	50	72	71	32	19	22	18	9	7
Reduce the number of counselors on the staff	32	52	49	49	38	42	19	10	9
Reduce the number of subjects offered	30	39	35	57	53	58	13	8	7
Cut out the 12th grade by covering in 3 years what is now covered in 4	29	36	31	58	58	62	13	6	7
Cut out after-school activities like bands, clubs, athletics, etc.	23	31	29	68	63	64	9	6	7
Reduce the number of teachers by increasing class sizes*	11	23	18	79	70	76	10	7	6
Cut all teachers' salaries by a set percentage	12	18	17	77	74	76	11	8	7
Reduce special services such as speech, reading, and hearing therapy	10	10	11	80	85	83	10	5	6
Reduce instruction in the basics—reading, writing, and arithmetic	—	—	3	—	—	93	—	—	4

*Gallup's interviewers do not give information to respondents. Thus they could not explain that teacher salaries typically constitute some 80% of a district's total operating expense. In many larger districts, increasing class size by one student could "save" more money than the elimination of 60% of the administrative staff.

Do you think that school buildings are more expensive than they need to be? (1969, 1972)

	1969 %	1972 %
Yes, in general	26	53
Yes, too fancy, too elaborate	14	—
No, in general	42	35
No, they are not good enough	7	—
DK	11	12

To utilize school buildings to the full extent, would you favor keeping the schools open the year around? Parents could choose which three of the four quarters of the year their children could attend. Do you approve or disapprove of this idea? (1970, 1972)

	1970 %	1972 %
Approve	42	53
Disapprove	49	41
DK	9	6

In order to save energy (fuel oil, gas), it has been suggested that the schools be closed in the middle of the winter. Children would make up lost school time by starting the school year in late August and ending the school year around the first of July. Would you favor or oppose adopting this plan here? (1977)

	%
Favor	36
Oppose	56
DK	8

Many schools are being closed today because of a drop in enrollment. What suggestions do you have as to how vacant school buildings might be used? (1978)

1. Community activities
2. Adult education centers
3. Vocational and job training
4. Cultural centers (museums, libraries, concerts, exhibitions, theaters)
5. Senior citizen centers
6. Youth activities
7. Make into offices
8. Use for governmental agencies
9. Sell or rent
10. Convert to apartments

One way which has been suggested to reduce school costs would be to interest local citizen volunteers to take over all extracurricular activities, such as athletic coaching, directing the band, directing plays, etc. Do you think this is a good idea or a bad idea? (1981)

	%
Good	52
Bad	41
DK	7

In some schools, teachers and students have fund-raising events to finance special projects for school equipment, after-school activities, and the like. Do you think it is a good idea or a poor idea for the schools to permit these events? (1971)

	%
Good	84
Poor	11
DK	5

Does your child bring money from home to pay for anything, except lunch, in school? (1971)(Asked only of parents of school children.)

	%
Yes	59
No	39
DK	2

If "Yes," for what? (1971)

	%
Books	9
Supplies for class (general)	7
Travel expenses for field trips	5
Athletic fees/equipment	3
School newspaper/school-related newspaper	3
Fees for special programs	3
Club dues/class dues	2
Parties/dances	2
Charitable contributions/events	2
General school activities	1
Miscellaneous	9

Do you think such fees should be charged? (1971)

	%
Yes	47
No	10
DK	2

Federal Government and the Schools

Department of Education

In your opinion, should education be taken out of the present Department of Health, Education, and Welfare and made a separate department of the federal government, or not? (1977)

	%
Favor	40
Oppose	45
DK	15

As you may know, a new federal Department of Education has been established with Cabinet status. We would like to know what you think this new department should give special attention to in the next five years. Will you choose five of the areas listed on this card which you think are most important? (1980)

	%
1. Basic education (reading, writing, arithmetic)	69
2. Vocational training (training students for jobs)	56
3. Improving teacher training and education	46
4. Helping students choose careers	46
5. Parent training to help parents become more fully involved in their children's education	45
6. Helping more students obtain a college education	35
7. Developing individual educational plans for every child	33
8. Providing more opportunities for gifted students	25
9. Preschool education	24
10. Lifelong learning (continuing education through adult life)	23
11. Better educational use of television	20
12. International education, including foreign language study	19
13. Improving opportunities for women and minorities	18

Two years ago a new Department of Education was established in the federal government in Washington, D.C. The present administration now says such a department is not needed and that its functions should be performed by a smaller agency or by other departments of the government. Do you agree or disagree with this view? (1981)

	%
Agree that DOE not needed	49
Disagree, is needed	29
DK	22

Federal Influence

Thinking about the future, would you like the federal government in Washington to have more influence, or less influence, in determining the educational program of the local public schools? (1982)

	%
More influence	28
Less influence	54
Same as now	10
DK	8

Some people worry that the state and the federal government are adopting many regulations regarding educational matters which don't take account of the local school situation. Do you think these actions by the state and the federal government are more likely to help, or more likely to hinder, public school education here? (1978)

	%
Help	23
Hinder	44
Make no difference	5
DK	28

Private and Parochial Schools

Reasons for Increase in Nonpublic Schools

In recent years the number of nonpublic schools, that is, private and church-related schools, has increased in many parts of the nation. Why do you think this has happened? (1981)

In order of times mentioned
1. Poor educational standards in the public schools; education in nonpublic schools is superior
2. Integration/forced busing/racial problems
3. Greater discipline in nonpublic schools
4. More attention given to religion in nonpublic schools.
5. Too many drug and alcohol problems in the public schools
6. Overcrowding in the public schools

Favor/Oppose Increase

In general, do you think this increase in nonpublic schools is a good thing or a bad thing for the nation? (1981)

	%
Increase in nonpublic schools is a good thing	49
Is a bad thing	30
DK	21

Government Tax Aid to Nonpublic Schools

It has been proposed that some government tax money be used to help parochial (church-related) schools make ends meet. How do you feel about this? Do you favor or oppose giving some government tax money to help parochial schools? (1970, 1981)

	1970 %	1981 %
Favor	48	40
Oppose	44	51
DK	8	9

These proposals are being suggested to amend the U.S. Constitution. As I read each one will you tell me if you favor or oppose it.

An amendment to the Constitution that would permit government financial aid to parochial schools? (1974)

	%
Favor	52
Oppose	35
DK	13

In some nations, the government allots a certain amount of money for each child for his education. The parents can then send the child to any public, parochial, or private school they choose. This is called the "voucher system." Would you like to see such an idea adopted in this country? (1970, 1971, 1981, 1983)

	1970 %	1971 %	1981 %	1983 %
Favor	43	38	43	51
Oppose	46	44	41	38
DK	11	18	16	11

Private Schools Versus Public Schools

Suppose you could send your eldest child to a private school, tuition free. Which would you prefer — to send him or her to a private school or to a public school? (1982) (Asked of parents of public school children.)

	%
Private school	45
Public school	47
DK	8

Why do you say that? (1982) (Asked of public school parents who said they would prefer private school if tuition free.)

	%
Higher standard of education	28
Better discipline	27
More individual attention	21
Smaller class size	17
Better curriculum	12
Quality of teachers	11
Religious/moral reasons	5
Parents have more input	3
Miscellaneous	10
DK	1

Curriculum

General Attitudes

Do you think the school curriculum in your community needs to be changed to meet today's needs or do you think it already meets today's needs? (1970, 1982)

	1970 %	1982 %
Needs to be changed	31	36
Already meets needs	46	42
DK	23	22

In what ways do you feel it needs to be changed? (1982) (Asked of those who answered "needs to be changed" to above question.)

	%
More emphasis on basics	26
More practical instruction	14
More vocational classes	11
Raise academic standards	8
Greater variety of classes	5
More computer courses	4
More math courses	3
More foreign language	3
Upgrade textbooks	3
Stress religion more	3
More English courses	2
More science courses	2
Remove sex education	1
More for gifted students	1
More arts	1
Better college preparation	1
Add health classes	1
Miscellaneous	5
DK	7

Now, thinking about your oldest child in school (elementary, junior, or senior high — not college): Do you think he (she) is learning the things you believe he (she) should be learning? (1973, 1983)

	1973 %	1983 %
Yes	81	74
No	14	20
DK	5	6

Decision on Curriculum

In your opinion, who should have the greatest influence in deciding what is taught in the public schools here — the federal government, the state government, or the local school board? (1980)

	%
Federal government	9
State government	15
Local school board	68
DK	8

Back to Basics

Have you heard or read about the back-to-basics movement in education? (1977)

	%
Yes	41
No	57
DK	2

Do you favor or oppose this back-to-basics movement? (1977) (Asked of those who were aware of the term.)

	%
Favor	83
Oppose	11
DK	6

When this term is used, do you think of anything besides reading, writing, and arithmetic? (1977)

The responses to this question, on the whole, indicate that the public regarded the basics largely in terms of the traditional three subject areas.

Other subjects were mentioned — history, geography, spelling, citizenship, science, music, art, physical education — but not frequently.

However, many respondents thought of the term, not in relation to subjects or courses, but in relation to the educational process itself. Thus, "back to basics" was interpreted as meaning a return to schooling of earlier years. To many respondents it meant "respect for teachers," "good manners," "politeness," "obedience," "respect for elders," "structured classrooms," "back to the old ways of teaching."

Is it your impression that the local public school system gives enough attention, or not enough attention, to reading, writing, and arithmetic? (1980) (Asked of all respondents with children in school.)

	Public School Parents %	Private School Parents %
Enough	34	17
Not enough	61	72
DK	5	11

Public high schools can offer students a wide variety of courses, or they can concentrate on fewer basic courses such as English, mathematics, history, and science. Which of these two policies do you think the local high school(s) should follow in planning their curriculum — a wide variety of courses or fewer but more basic courses? (1979, 1981)

	1979 %	1981 %
Favor a wide variety	44	43
Favor fewer, basic courses	49	52
DK	7	5

Which three of these educational programs (card lists) would you like your local elementary school (grades 1-6) to give more attention to? Junior and senior high schools (grades 7-12)? (1972)

	Rank Order Elementary	Jr. & Sr. High School
Teaching students the skills of reading, writing, and arithmetic	1	7
Teaching students how to solve problems and think for themselves	2	2
Teaching students to respect law and authority	3	1
Teaching students how to get along with others	4	4
Teaching students the skills of speaking and listening	5	5
Teaching students vocational skills	6	3
Teaching students health and physical education	7	8
Teaching students about the world of today and yesterday (that is, history, geography, and civics)	8	6
Teaching students how to compete with others	9	9

Subjects Required

Would you look over this card which lists high school subjects. If you were the one to decide, what subjects would you require every public high school student who plans to go on to college to take? (1981, 1983)

	1981 Would Require %	1981 Number Years Required	1983 Would Require %
Mathematics	94	4	92
English	91	4	88
History/U.S. gov't	83	4	76
Science	76	4	76
Business	60	2	55
Foreign language	54	2	50
Health education	47	1 to 2	43
Physical education	44	1 to 2	41
Industrial arts/homemaking	34	2	32
Art	28	2	19
Music	26	1	18

What about those public high school students who do *not plan to go to college* when they graduate. Which courses would you require them to take? (1981, 1983)

	1981 Would Require %	1981 Number Years Required	1983 Would Require %
Mathematics	91	4	87
English	89	4	83
Business	75	4	65
History/U.S. gov't	71	2	63
Vocational training	64	4	74
Science	58	2	53
Health education	46	2	42
Physical education	43	4	40
Foreign language	21	2	19
Art	20	1	16
Music	20	1	16

(If foreign language) What foreign language or languages should be required? (1983)

	%
Spanish	56
French	34
German	16
Latin	8
Russian	8
Japanese	6
Other	4
DK	24

Special Instruction Requirements

In addition to regular courses, high schools offer instruction in other areas. As I read off these areas, one at a time, would you tell me whether you feel this instruction should be required or should not be required for all high school students. (1981, 1983) (Percentages are for those who responded "should be required.")

	1981 %	1983 %
Drug abuse	82	81
Alcohol abuse	78	76
Driver education	71	72
Computer training	43	72
Parenting/parent training	64	58
Dangers of nuclear waste	*	56
Race relations	*	56
Communism/socialism	*	51
Dangers of nuclear war	*	46

*Not included in 1981 list

Essential Subjects

Public schools can teach many different things. Will you tell me, in the case of each of these high school subjects, whether you regard it as essential for all students, or not too essential? (1979)

	Essential %	Not Too Essential %	DK %
Mathematics	97	1	2
English grammar and composition	94	3	3
Civics, government	88	8	4
U.S. history	86	11	3
Science	83	14	3
Geography	81	16	3
Physical education	76	21	3
Interdependence of nations, foreign rel.	60	32	8
Music	44	52	4
Foreign language	43	53	4
Art	37	58	5

Sex Education

Do you approve or disapprove of schools giving courses in sex education? (1970)

	%
Approve	65
Disapprove	28
DK	7

Would you approve or disapprove if these courses discussed birth control? (1970)

	%
Approve	56
Disapprove	35
DK	9

Do you feel the public *high* schools should or should not include sex education in their instructional program? ... the public *elementary* schools? (1981)

	Should %	Should Not %	DK %
High schools	70	22	8
Elementary schools	45	48	7

**1981
Topics That Should Be Included
(Responses of Parents Who Favor Sex Education)**

	In High School %	In Elementary School %
1. Venereal disease	85	46
2. Birth control	77	38
3. The biology of reproduction	78	85
4. Premarital sex	59	30
5. Abortion	52	20
6. Nature of sexual intercourse	48	35
7. Homosexuality	40	19

**1981
Topics That Should Be Included
(Responses of All Those Who Favor Sex Education)**

	In High School %	In Elementary School %
1. Venereal disease	84	52
2. Birth control	79	45
3. The biology of reproduction	77	83
4. Premarital sex	60	40
5. Abortion	54	26
6. Nature of sexual intercourse	53	36
7. Homosexuality	45	23

Science and Technology

Some observers say that the United States is losing its lead in science and technology to Japan and Germany. Do you think this is true or not true? (1981)

	%
U.S. losing	48
U.S. not losing	38
DK	14

Ethics and Values

Would you favor or oppose instruction in the schools that would deal with values and ethical behavior? (1975, 1981)

	1975*	1981
	%	%
Favor	79	70
Oppose	15	17
DK	6	13

*Words used in 1975 were "morals and moral behavior."

Parents now have responsibility for the moral behavior of their children. Do you think that the schools should take on a share of this responsibility, or not? (1976)

	%
Should	67
Should not	30
DK	3

School Prayers

These proposals are being suggested to amend the U.S. Constitution. As I read each one, will you tell me if you favor or oppose it:

An amendment to the Constitution that would permit prayers to be said in the public schools. (1974)

	%
Favor	77
Oppose	17
DK	6

Citizenship Education

Young people who reach the age of 18 now have the right to vote. The question arises as to whether high school courses give students enough information about the Constitution, about government and the political process, to enable them to vote intelligently. What is your impression — how good a job do the schools perform in this respect: good, fair, or poor? (1974)

	%
Good	33
Fair	33
Poor	16
DK	18

International Citizenship

Should students spend more time than they now do learning about other nations of the world and the way people live there, or do you think they spend enough time now? (1980)

	%
More time	45
Enough now	46
DK	9

English for Non-English-Speaking

Many families who come from other countries have children who cannot speak English. Should or should not these children be required to learn English in special classes before they are enrolled in the public schools? (1980)

	%
Yes	82
No	13
DK	5

Other Innovations

In some schools, time spent by students in classrooms is being reduced to give more time for independent study, that is, carrying out learning projects on their own. Should the local schools give more time to independent study than they presently do, or should they give less time? (1971)

	%
More	31
Less	22
About right	25
DK	22

A plan has been suggested to enable all juniors and seniors in high school to perform some kind of community service for course credit — such as working in a hospital or recreation center, beautifying parks, or helping law enforcement officers. Would you like to have such a plan adopted in this community, or not? (1978)

	%
Yes	87
No	8
DK	5

Vocational Education

Do you think that the school curriculum should give more emphasis or less emphasis to careers and career preparation in high school? (1976)

	%
More	80
Less	5
Same	11
DK	4

Some people feel that too much emphasis is placed in the high schools on preparing students for college and not enough emphasis on preparing students for occupations that do not require a college degree. Do you agree or disagree? (1971)

	%
Agree	68
Disagree	23
DK	9

		%
Should public schools give more emphasis to a study of trades, professions, and businesses to help students decide on their careers? (1973)	Yes	90
	No	7
	DK	3

		%
Do you think the *elementary* school curriculum should, or should not, include information about jobs and careers? (1976)	Should	52
	Should not	39
	DK	9

		%
In your opinion, should vocational education be separated from the school and conducted in a separate location by other agencies such as business or industry? (1978)	Yes	32
	No	53
	DK	15

Parents' Experience: Most Valuable Subjects

What subjects that you studied or experiences that you gained in high school have you found to be most useful in later life? (1978)

Subjects in Order of Times Mentioned
1. English
2. Mathematics
3. Commercial subjects
4. Extracurricular activities
5. Shop
6. History
7. Science
8. Foreign language
9. Psychology
10. Domestic science

And now thinking only of the subjects that were offered in your high school, are there any subjects you *wish* you had studied and didn't that would be of special help to you now? (1978)

Subjects in Order of Times Mentioned
1. Typing and other secretarial skills
2. Mathematics
3. Shop
4. Foreign languages
5. Science
6. English
7. History
8. Civics
9. Home Economics
10. Music

Graduation Requirements

What requirements, if any, would you set for graduation from high school for those students who do *not* plan to go on to college but who plan to take a job or job training following graduation? I'll read off a number of requirements and then you tell me how important each one is as a requirement for graduation for these students. We would like to know whether you think it is very important, fairly important, or not important. (1975, 1978)

How important is it that these students..	Very Important % 1975	Very Important % 1978	Fairly Important % 1975	Fairly Important % 1978	Not Important % 1975	Not Important % 1978	DK % 1975	DK % 1978
...be able to write a letter of application using correct grammar and correct spelling?	92	90	6	9	1	*	1	1
...be able to read well enough to follow an instruction manual for home appliances?	96	86	3	12	*	1	1	1
...know enough arithmetic to be able to figure out such a problem as the total square feet in a room?	87	84	10	14	2	1	1	1
...know the health hazards of smoking and the use of alcohol, marijuana, and other drugs?	†	83	†	14	†	2	†	1
...have a salable skill, such as typing, auto mechanics, nurse's aide, business machines?	85	79	12	17	2	3	1	1
...know something about the U.S. government, the political parties, voting procedures?	75	66	21	30	3	3	1	1
...know something about the history of the U.S., such as the Constitution, Bill of Rights, and the like?	68	61	27	31	4	7	1	1
...know something about the major nations of the world today, their kind of government, and their way of life?	49	42	40	46	10	10	1	2
...know something about the history of mankind, the great leaders in art, literature?	33	30	44	48	21	21	2	1
...know a foreign language?	18	16	28	32	51	50	3	2

* Less than 1%
† Not asked in 1975

Computers

Availability

Does the school your child attends have a computer that students can use? (1983)

	Public School Parents %	Nonpublic School Parents %
Yes	45	47
No	32	33
DK	23	20

(If no) Would you like the school your child attends to install a computer that students could use? (1983)

	Public School Parents %	Nonpublic School Parents %
Yes	81	56
No	10	30
DK	9	14

Who Should Choose Instructional Material/Books?

When parents object to books or materials in textbooks on grounds of religion, politics, race, or sex discrimination, how much consideration should be given to the parents' view in deciding whether to keep these books in the school — a great deal, some, little, or none? (1975)

	%
A great deal	33
Some	43
Little	12
None	7
DK	5

Who do you feel should have the most influence in the selection of books for use in the public school classrooms and school libraries — the parents, the school board, the teachers, or the principals and school administrators? (1982)

	%
Teachers	42
Parents	18
Principals and school administrators	15
School boards	13
DK	12

Schoolwork and Homework

Working Hard/Not Hard Enough

In general, do you think elementary school children in the public schools here are made to work too hard in school and on homework, or not hard enough? . . . high school? (1975, 1983)

Elementary	1975 %	1983 %
Too hard	5	4
Not hard enough	49	61
About right amount	28	19
DK	18	16

High School	1975 %	1983 %
Too hard	3	3
Not hard enough	54	65
About right amount	22	12
DK	21	20

An educator claims that children are not achieving as well in school today as they did 20 years ago because they are given about one-third less work to do in school and after school. Do you think children are assigned less work today? (1979)

	Public School Parents %	Parochial School Parents %
Yes	51	59
No	38	22
DK	11	19

Parental Help on Homework

Do you regularly help your child with his/her homework? (1977)

	Public School Parents %	Parochial School Parents %
Yes, regularly	24	17
Yes, when he/she needs help	27	32
No	44	41
DK	5	10

When the age of the eldest child is considered, parents respond in this way:

	Children 12 Years of Age And Under %	Children 13 Years of Age And Older %
Yes, regularly	37	16
Yes, when he/she needs help	34	26
No	27	58
DK	2	*

* Less than 1%

As a parent, how much time do you usually have to devote to your youngster in the evening to assist him/her with his/her homework — enough time, not enough time, or none at all? (1978)

	%
Enough	64
Not enough	17
None	13
DK	6

Time Limit on TV Viewing

Do you place definite limits on the amount of time your eldest child spends viewing television during the school week? (1977, 1981)

	Yes 1977 %	Yes 1981 %
National Totals	35	36
Parents whose oldest child is 12 or under	49	51
Parents whose oldest child is 13 or older	28	27
Parents of child in upper half of class	*	41
Parents of child in lower half of class	*	34

* Not asked in 1977.

Extracurricular Activities

Perceived Importance

I'd like your opinion about extracurricular activities such as the school band, dramatics, sports, the school paper. How important are these to a young person's education — very important, fairly important, not too important, or not at all important? (1978)

	%
Very important	45
Fairly important	40
Not too important	9
Not all all important	4
DK	2

Athletics

Do you think too much, too little, or about the right amount of emphasis is being given to athletics in the public high schools in this community? (1981)

	%
Too much emphasis	34
Too little	10
Right amount	49
DK	7

Girls' Sports

Should girls have equal financial support for their athletic activities as boys? (1974)

	%
Yes	88
No	7
DK	5

Should girls be permitted to participate in noncontact sports — track, tennis, golf, baseball, and the like — on the same teams with boys? (1974)

	%
Yes	59
No	35
DK	6

The federal government may require all high schools to spend the same amount of money on women's sports as on men's sports. Do you approve or disapprove of this plan? (1979)

	%
Approve	61
Disapprove	29
DK	10

Testing

Tests for Grade Promotion

In your opinion, should children be promoted from grade to grade *only* if they can pass examinations? (1978, 1983)

	1978 %	1983 %
Yes	68	75
No	27	20
DK	5	5

National Achievement Tests

Would you like to see the students in the local schools be given national tests so that their educational achievement could be compared with students in other communities? (1970, 1971, 1983)

	1970 %	1971 %	1983 %
Yes	75	70	75
No	16	21	17
DK	9	9	8

Do you think the students here would get higher scores then students in similar communities, or not so high? (1970)

	%
Higher	21
Not so high	15
Same	44
DK	20

Some people believe that since every community has a different racial and occupational mix, tests given in different subjects for promotion should be prepared for that school system only. Other people think the tests should be prepared on a statewide basis. Still others think that they should be prepared on a national basis to be given to students in the same grade throughout the nation. Which of these three ways would you prefer — having tests prepared on a local, state, or national basis? (1978)

	%
Local	37
State	25
National	28
DK	10

Should students who fail be required to take special remedial classes in the subjects they fail or should they be required to repeat the whole year's work? (1978)

	%
Yes, special classes	81
No, repeat whole year	14
DK	5

What do you think should be done with students who do not pass the examinations even *after* they have received extra instruction? (1978) (Open-end)

The public was divided on the policies to be followed, with about half saying that in this situation the child should repeat the grade and the rest suggesting further help or placing the child in a special program.

An interesting aspect of the public's views on automatic promotion comes to light in an examination of the groups who supported and those who opposed automatic or social promotion. Those who were most likely to have children who fail in their schoolwork — poorly educated parents — were the ones most in favor of requiring students to pass tests for promotion. At the other extreme, persons who had completed high school or college were most in favor of automatic or social promotion.

Early Graduation from High School

If high school students can meet academic requirements in three years instead of four, should they, or should they not, be permitted to graduate early? (1977, 1980)

	1977 %	1980 %
Yes, should	74	77
No, should not	22	19
DK	4	4

For High School Diploma

Should all high school students in the United States be required to pass a standard *nationwide* examination in order to get a high school diploma? (1976, 1981)

	1958* %	1976 %	1981 %
Favor	50	65	69
Oppose	39	31	26
DK	11	4	5

*The Gallup Organization asked this question before the annual education polls were started in 1969.

As an aid to interpreting these results, do you feel the results for each school should or should not show how their results compare with other schools that have a similar racial and economic make-up? (1981)

	%
Yes, compare	91
No	7
DK	2

Do you feel that the results of a nationwide examination should, or should not, be released to the press and made public? (1981)

	%
Yes, should	53
No	43
DK	4

Decline in National Test Scores

Do you believe that a decline in national test scores of students in recent years means that the quality of education today is declining? (1976)

	%
Yes	59
No	31
DK	10

The national tests that have been given to students throughout the nation indicate that students today do not have as high scores as they had a few years ago in many subject areas. What do you think is the reason for this? (Open-end) (1975)

	%
Students' lack of interest/motivation	29
Lack of discipline in the home and school	28
Poor curriclum (too easy, not enough emphasis on basics)	22
Inadequate teachers, uninterested teachers	21
Too many outside interests, including TV	8
Miscellaneous, including integration, overcrowding, drugs, etc.	13
DK	13

Here are some reasons that have been given to explain the decline in national test scores. Will you look over these reasons and then tell me which ones you think are most responsible for this decline? (Respondent shown card) (1976)

	%
Less parent attention, concern, and supervision of the child	65
Students aren't as motivated to do well	52
Too much television viewing	49
Society is becoming too permissive	49
Teachers are giving less attention to students	39
It's easier to get into college now	16
Schools are expanding the number of courses offered	10
The tests are not reliable	16
Other and DK	14

School Attendance

Absenteeism/Truancy

In some of our schools, absenteeism is as high as 40% on a given day. In your opinion, should those students who are frequently absent *without good reason* be dismissed from school, or should they be forced to attend? (1978)

	%
Should be dismissed	19
Should be forced to attend	63
No action should be taken	6
DK	12

Should or should not parents be held responsible for their children's school attendance? (1978)

	%
Parents responsible	86
Parents not responsible	6
DK	8

In your opinion, should, or should not, parents be brought into court and given a small fine when a child of theirs is frequently absent without excuse (truant) from school? (1977)

	%
Yes, should fine	51
No	40
DK	9

In your opinion, what can be done by the schools to reduce student absenteeism (truancy)? (1977) (Open-end)

The suggestions offered tend to fall in about equal numbers into three broad categories.

Category 1 — Persons who, in general, believe that the schools and the teachers are chiefly to blame for absenteeism.

These typical direct quotations indicate how persons in this category would deal with the problem: "The courses should be made more interesting. Few teachers ever bother to make what they are teaching exciting or important to the students." "Teachers should spend more time with students, be more dedicated, and avoid being clock watchers." "Courses should be more practical, more 'today'-related." "Get the students who stay away from school most often to sit down and talk over their school problems and make their own suggestions about solving the problem." "Incentives should be devised.... Have each class compete with other classes. The one with the highest attendance gets a half-day off."

Category 2 — Persons who, in general, start with the conviction that parents are chiefly to blame for absenteeism.

Some of their suggestions follow: "Parents, whether they are at home or work, should be immediately notified if their child fails to show up at school." "Parents in many cases do not realize how important attendance is. They should be brought together and told exactly why attendance is so important." "When a child stays away from school the parents should be made to confer with the teachers, with the child present, to find out why." "The schools and the local authorities should get after the parents. Put them on the block and make them see that they are responsible."

Category 3 — Persons who, in general, regard truancy as a matter for the police and local authorities.

Some typical suggestions: "More truant officers should be hired and local laws should be strictly enforced." "The police should be ordered to stop any child of school age who is on the streets during school hours. If the child doesn't have a written excuse, he or she should be taken into custody."

Other suggestions: "Children who are frequently absent should have to obey earlier curfew laws." "They should have to make up their schoolwork on Saturdays or during summer vacation." "They should be put to work cleaning up the parks and playgrounds."

Parent's Experience

About how many days has your child (the eldest now in school) been absent since school opened last September? (1979)

	%
0 to 5 days	56
6 to 10 days	21
11 to 15 days	9
16 to 20 days	3
21 days & over	4
DK	7

Do you think it is possible for your child to be absent without your knowledge? (1979)

	Yes %	No %	DK %
Parents whose eldest child is 12 years or under	15	84	1
Parents whose eldest child is 13 years or over	47	53	–

Does the school let you know promptly about each absence? (1979)

	Yes %	No %	DK %
Parents whose eldest child is 12 years or under	50	37	13
Parents whose eldest child is 13 years or over	57	36	7

Compulsory Attendance

In each state children are required to go to school until they reach a certain age. If you were the one to decide, what would be the age? (1972)

	%
14 & under	2
15 years	1
16 years	28
Over 16 years	61
DK	8

Do you believe those youngsters not interested in school should be forced to attend elementary school (grades 1 to 6)? . . . Junior and senior high school (grades 7 to 12)? (1972)

	Elementary %	High School %
Yes	91	73
No	7	24
DK	2	3

Currently some states are considering legislation which will permit students to leave school as early as age 14 if they can first pass a test showing that they can read, write, and figure with sufficient skill to get along. Those who pass the test and leave school can take jobs if they wish or go on to community college at an earlier age. Do you approve or disapprove of such a plan for letting students leave school at a younger age? (1976)

	%
Approve	30
Disapprove	66
DK	4

Age for Starting School

Some educators have proposed that young children start school a year earlier, at the age of 4. Does this sound like a good idea or not? (1972, 1973)

	1972 %	1973 %
Favor	32	30
Oppose	64	64
DK	4	6

Length of School Year, Day

In some nations, students attend school as many as 240 days a year as compared to about 180 days in the U.S. How do you feel about extending the public school year in this community by 30 days, making the school year about 210 days or 10 months long? Do you favor or oppose this idea? (1982, 1983)

	1982 %	1983 %
Favor	37	40
Oppose	53	49
DK	10	11

How do you feel about extending the school day in the public schools in this community by one hour? Do you favor or oppose this idea? (1982, 1983)

	1982 %	1983 %
Favor	37	41
Oppose	55	48
DK	8	11

The Uninterested Student

Perceptions of Own Child's Interest

Just how much or how little does your (eldest) child enjoy going to school — very much, somewhat, or very little? (1979)

	%
Very much	60
Somewhat	28
Very little	8
DK	4

Is he (she) happy to go to school — that is, does he (she) go to school because he (she) wants to go, or simply because he (she) is required to attend? (1973)

	%
Wants to go	83
Goes because it is required	14
DK	3

Now, I would like to ask you something about *one* of your children — the oldest of your children who is now attending school. Could anything be done by the school to increase your child's interest in going to school? (1972)

	Public School Parents %	Private School Parents %
Yes	42	30
No	46	51
DK	12	19

Some students are not interested in school. Often they keep other students from working in school. What should be done in these cases? (1971) (open-end)

	%
Special classes for all who are not interested	29
Expel them	12
Offer better/more interesting curriculum/teaching methods	11
Special counseling	9
Harsher discipline	9
Vocational training	8
Make their parents responsible	7
Put in a school for problem students	6
Teachers should take more interest in such students	4
Miscellaneous	5
DK	18

Some students have no interest in school work as now offered in junior and senior high school and they become a problem. Here are some ways that have been proposed for dealing with these students. Will you tell me in the case of each proposal whether or not you approve of it? (1974) (aided)

	Approve %	Disapprove %	DK %
Special training courses	94	4	2
Work-study	86	9	5
Credit for volunteer work	77	17	6
Special programs for out-of-the-ordinary students	79	14	7
Job training	74	21	5
Permit students to quit	18	78	4

Asked of High School Juniors and Seniors

What would make school more interesting and useful to you? (1974)

	%
Wider variety of subjects	35
Better/more interested teachers	14
Extracurricular activities	10
Freedom to choose courses	8
Better preparation for non-college students	8
Better facilities	6
More free time	6
Better student/teacher relationships	3
Open classrooms	2
Better relationships between students	1
Miscellaneous	6
Nothing — it's all right now	8
DK	10

If you could get a good full-time job, would you prefer taking the job or would you prefer to continue going to school? (1974)

	%
Job	22
School	78

The Handicapped Student

Support for Mainstreaming

Should physically handicapped children be put in the same classrooms with other students, or should they be put in special classes of their own? ... Mentally handicapped? (1979)

	Handicapped	
	Physically %	Mentally %
Same classes	53	13
Special classes	36	77
DK	11	10

Who Should Pay

Services for the physically and mentally handicapped student cost more than regular school services. When the local schools are required to provide these special services by the federal government, should the federal government pay the extra cost, or not? (1977)

	%
Federal government should pay	82
Should not pay	11
DK	7

The Special Student

Special Instruction for Students With Learning Problems

How do you feel about the spending of public school funds for special instruction and homework programs for students with *learning problems*? Do you feel that more public school funds should be spent on students with learning problems than on average students — or the same amount? (1982)

	%
More spent	42
Same amount spent	48
Less spent	4
DK	6

Special Instruction for Students Who Are Gifted and Talented

How do you feel about the spending of public school funds for special instruction and homework programs for *gifted and talented students*? Do you feel that more school funds should be spent on gifted and talented students than on average students — or the same amount? (1982)

	%
More spent	19
Same amount spent	64
Less spent	11
DK	6

Academic Self-Evaluation by High School Juniors and Seniors

How would you appraise your ability to convey your thoughts in writing? Read with speed and comprehension? Speak correctly, fluently, effectively? Develop new ideas, new solutions? (1970)

	Excellent %	Above Average %	Average %	Below Average %	Poor %
Convey your thoughts in writing	7	28	60	4	1
Read with speed and comprehension	5	34	48	12	1
Speak correctly, fluently, effectively	7	28	57	8	—
Develop new ideas, new solutions	8	35	50	7	—

Would you say that your vocabulary is excellent, above average, average, below average, poor? (1970)

Excellent %	Above Average %	Average %	Below Average %	Poor %
4	26	62	8	—

Discipline

Parents' Definitions

When we talk about "discipline" in the schools, just what does this mean to you? (1973, 1982) (open-end)

1973

The following statements convey some idea of the wide range of views:

"Discipline is respect for the teacher on the part of the child; and respect for the child on the part of the teacher."

"Learning taking place without confusion."

"Keeping children so interested in what they are learning that obeying the rules is almost automatic."

"Discipline is self-control and a proper respect for other students, for those in authority."

"Without discipline neither school nor society can exist. The world would be bedlam."

"Proper discipline makes children happier. When they run wild, they are undone by the confusion they create."

Most respondents saw discipline as a matter of obeying rules, respecting views of parents, teachers, and others in authority, and being considerate of fellow students who wish to learn in a peaceful atmosphere.

While law and order have become almost code words for the conservative viewpoint in politics, the basic concept is held in high regard by the public. In fact, in the 1972 survey, when asked to choose from a list of nine goals of education, the public placed "teaching students to respect law and authority" as the top goal for students in grades 7-12.

1982

	%
Obeying rules/regulations	54
Authority/control by teachers	31
Respect for teachers	18
Students' lack of willingness to learn	7
Fighting/violence	3
Smoking/drugs	2
Miscellaneous	1
DK	5

How Serious

How serious a problem would you say discipline is in the public schools in this community — very serious, fairly serious, not too serious, or not at all serious? (1982)

	National Totals %	No Children in School %	Public School Parents %	Nonpublic School Parents %
Very serious	39	39	37	46
Fairly serious	31	31	32	31
Not too serious	20	18	25	18
Not at all serious	2	2	4	2
DK	8	10	2	3

Discipline Too Strict

How do you feel about the discipline in the local schools — is it too strict, not strict enough, or just about right? (1969-1971)

	1969 %	1970 %	1971 %
Too strict	2	2	3
Not strict enough	49	53	48
Just about right	44	31	33
DK	5	14	16

(Asked of those who answered "not strict enough") Can you tell me what you mean? In what ways is discipline not strict enough? (1971)

	%
Teachers lack authority to keep order	11
Students have too much freedom; they can get away with anything	11
Students have no respect for their teachers; pay no attention to them	6
Rules are not enforced	3
Vandalism	2
Other and DK	11

(Asked of those who answered "not strict enough") Who should assume more responsibility for correcting this situation? (1970)

	%
Teachers	16
School administrators	16
Parents	30
School board	6
Students	2
Other	2
DK	2

Who Should Deal with Behavior Problems?

Here are some student behavior problems which may occur in school. In your opinion, who should deal with each kind of problem — should it be the parents, the school, or the courts? (1980)

	*Parents %	School %	Courts %	DK %
Truancy (skipping school)	72	45	9	2
Vandalism of school property	44	39	50	2
Bringing weapons to school	41	35	59	3
Fighting in school	42	75	10	3
Using alcohol or drugs on school property	50	57	35	2
Striking a teacher	43	56	35	3
Stealing money or clothing from other students	48	58	30	3

* Multiple answers permitted.

Causes of Disciplinary Problems

Many people say that discipline is one of the major problems of the public schools today. Would you please look over this list and tell me which reasons you think are most important to explain why there is a discipline problem? (1983)

	%
Lack of discipline in the home	72
Lack of respect for law and authority throughout society	54
Students who are constant troublemakers often can't be removed from school	42
Some teachers are not properly trained to deal with discipline problems	42
The courts have made school administrators so cautious that they don't deal severely with student misbehavior	41
Viewing television programs that emphasize crime and violence	39
Punishment is too lenient	39
Decline in the teaching of good manners	37
Teachers themselves do not command respect	36
Failure on the part of teachers to make classroom work more interesting	31
One-parent families	26

How to Improve Situation

Some people say that if the schools and the teachers interest the children in learning, most disciplinary problems disappear. Do you agree or disagree? (1971)

	%
Agree	76
Disagree	18
DK	6

55

Punishment

Spanking and similar forms of physical punishment are permitted in the lower grades of some schools for children who do not respond to other forms of discipline. Do you approve or disapprove of this practice? (1970)

	%
Approve	62
Disapprove	33
DK	5

What should be done with a high school student who refuses to obey his teacher? (1974)

	%
Punitive Action:	
Suspend/expel	31
Punish	11
Detention time	4
Paddle	7
Rehabilitation:	
Counsel	13
Provide work/study program	1
Discussion with principal, teacher, juvenile authorities	8
Involve parents	22
Provide special curriculum/teachers	10
Miscellaneous	3
DK	10

Supreme Court Decision

A U.S. Supreme Court decision requires school principals to give written notice to a student and his parents and to hold a hearing when the student is suspended from school. Have you heard or read about this ruling? (1975)

	%
Yes, heard	41
No	55
DK	4

Do you think the Court went too far in making this ruling? (1975) (Asked of those who had read or heard of the decision.)

	%
Yes, too far	26
No	67
DK	7

Financial Responsibility

Should parents be made financially responsible, or not, for damage to school property done by their children? (1978)

	%
Yes, should	86
No	11
DK	3

Dress Code

Some people feel the schools do not go far enough in regulating the way boys and girls dress for school. Do you think there should be greater regulation of the way children dress for school, or less? (1969)

	%
Greater	53
Less	7
OK as is	36
DK	4

Drugs, Alcohol, and Smoking

Drug Problems

Marijuana and other drugs are increasingly being used by students. Do you think it is a serious problem in your public schools? (1970)

Is the use of drugs by young people a serious problem in this community? (1975)

From what you have heard or read, is the use of marijuana by students enrolled in junior high (middle school) or high school here a serious problem, or not? (1978)

Serious Problem

	In Public School 1970 %	In Community 1975 %	In Junior High or High School 1978 %
Yes	64	58	66
No	22	27	20
DK	14	15	14

What about hard drugs (heroin, cocaine, etc.)? Is it a serious problem among [junior or senior high school] students here, or not? (1978)

	%
Yes	35
No	41
DK	24

Schools Teaching About Drugs

Do you feel that the local public schools are doing a good job of teaching the bad effects of drug use? (1970)

	%
Yes	39
No	25
DK	36

Alcohol Problems

What about use of alcohol (beer, wine, liquor) by students here? Is it a serious problem, or not? (1978)

	%
Yes	64
No	19
DK	17

What about alcoholic drinks? (Is it a serious problem among young people in this community?) (1975)

	%
Yes	55
No	27
DK	18

Should the schools in this community require students to attend a program on the effects of drugs and alcohol? (1975)

	%
Yes	84
No	11
DK	5

Smoking

How do you feel about smoking in public school buildings and on public school property? Do you feel that students should be prohibited from smoking in these places or not?... teachers, administrative staff? (1981)

	Students %	Teachers and Administrative Staff %
Yes, prohibit	71	60
No	25	34
DK	4	6

Crime

Prevalence

From what you have heard or read, is it your impression that stealing (money, clothes, lunches, books, etc.) goes on a great deal, some, or very little in the local public schools? (1974)

	%
Goes on a great deal	33
Some	34
Very little	15
DK	18

Are student gangs that disrupt the school or bother other students a big problem, somewhat of a problem, or not a problem in the local public schools? (1974)

	%
Big problem	17
Somewhat of a problem	31
Not a problem	32
DK	20

Fear for Child

When your child is outside at play in your own neighborhood, do you fear for his/her safety? (1977)

When he/she is at school, do you fear for his/her physical safety? (1977)

	In Own Neighborhood		At School	
	Public School Parents %	Parochial School Parents %	Public School Parents %	Parochial School Parents %
Yes	28	30	25	19
No	68	61	69	73
DK	4	9	6	8

Juvenile Courts

In your opinion, how good a job do the juvenile courts do here in dealing with young people who violate the law — an excellent job, a fair job or a poor job? (1976)

	%
Excellent job	6
Fair job	37
Poor job	41
DK	16

Student Rights

Too Many/Not Enough

Generally speaking, do the local public school students in this community have too many rights and privileges, or not enough? (1972, 1975)

	1972 %	1975 %
Too many	41	45
Just right	11	27
Not enough	33	10
DK	15	18

Should high school students have more say about what goes on within the school on matters such as curriculum? ... teachers? ... school rules? ... student dress? (1970)

	Yes %	No %	DK %
Curriculum	38	53	9
Teachers	22	72	6
School rules	36	58	6
School dress	37	57	6

Should students who are 18 years of age, and now have the right to vote, have more rights and privileges than other students? (1972)

	%
Yes	21
No	73
DK	6

Demonstrations

Have there been any demonstrations protesting school policies or procedures in your public schools during this present school year? (1970)

	%
Yes	19
No	64
DK	17

Integration and Racial Issues

Perceived Reasons People Move to Suburbs

As you know, many families living in the big cities of the nation are moving to the suburbs. Why, in your opinion, are they doing this? (1973)

	%
Big city congestion	37
Fear of high crime level	24
Less pollution	17
To get away from minorities	14
Better educational opportunities	12
More open spaces	11
More desirable housing	11
Better environment for children	9
Cities are too noisy	7
DK	6
High city taxes	6
Deterioration of the big cities	4
Miscellaneous	4
Lack of privacy	3
To create friendships	3
Improve one's standard of living	3
Lower rental costs	2
Lower cost of living in suburbs	2
Better employment opportunities	1
Children get in more trouble in cities	1
Drug problem	1
Status symbol	1

Perceived Educational Opportunities

Do you think that students from all racial groups have equal *educational* opportunity in this community? (1981)

	%
Yes	79
No	15
DK	6

In your opinion, do black children and other minorities in this community have the same educational opportunities as white children? (1975)

	%
Yes	80
No	14
DK	6

School Integration

Now, a question about how you feel about school integration. Do you believe more should be done — or less should be done — to integrate the schools throughout the nation? (1973)

	%
More	30
Less	38
No change	23
DK	9

How do you feel about school integration? Do you feel it has improved the quality of education received by black students? ... white students? (1971)

	Blacks %	Whites %
Yes	43	23
No	31	51
DK	26	26

Do you feel it (school integration) has improved relations between blacks and whites or has it worked against better relations? (1971)

	%
Improved	40
Worked against	35
DK	25

Busing

Do you favor busing of school children for the purpose of racial integration, or should busing for this purpose be prohibited through a constitutional amendment? (1974)

	%
Favor	18
Prohibit	72
DK	10

Parental/Citizen Involvement

Citizen Advisory Committees

Some school boards have appointed citizen advisory committees to deal with a number of school problems such as discipline, the curriculum, textbook selection, teacher evaluation, the athletic program, and the like. The committees report their findings to the school board for possible action. If such a plan were adopted here (or exists here), which of these problems would *you* most like to deal with on a citizen advisory committee? (1976)

		Percent Who Would Like to Serve on Such a Committee %
1.	Discipline and related problems	47
2.	Student/teacher relations	31
3.	Career education	29
4.	Student dropouts	29
5.	Teacher evaluation	28
6.	The handicapped student	26
7.	Educational costs and finances	22
8.	The curriculum	21
9.	Education for citizenship	19
10.	Work/study programs	19
11.	Home study and work habits	19
12.	Community use of school buildings	16
13.	Pupil assessment and test results	15
14.	School facilities	14
15.	Public relations of schools	13
16.	School transportation	12
17.	The athletic program	12
18.	Educational innovations	12
19.	Extracurricular activities	11
20.	Progress of recent graduates	9
	None	4
	DK	6

Many school systems have committees made up of citizens who serve in an advisory capacity. Do you think these advisory groups should have the final decision-making authority over the *curriculum*, or should the final authority remain with the school board? ... staff selection? ... budget? (1977)

	Curriculum %	Staff Selection %	Budget %
Citizen group	17	15	19
School board	71	75	70
DK	12	10	11

Parental Influence

Do you feel that parents of public school students should have more say, less say, or do they have about the right amount of say about the following areas in the public schools? (1981)

	More Say %	Less Say %	Right Amount %	DK %
1. The curriculum, i.e., the courses offered	38	8	43	11
2. The selection and hiring of teachers	34	14	41	11
3. The selection and hiring of administrators and principals	41	13	35	11
4. The books and instructional materials	37	10	41	12
5. The books placed in the school libraries	33	10	43	14
6. Teacher and administrator salaries	31	11	43	15

Classes for Parents

A suggestion has been made that parents of school children attend one evening class a month to find out what they can do at home to improve their children's behavior and increase their interest in school work. Is it a good idea or a poor idea? (1971)

	%
Good idea	81
Poor idea	13
DK	6

As a regular part of the public school educational system, it has been suggested that courses be offered at convenient times to parents in order to help them help their children in school. Do you think this is a good idea or a poor idea? (1976)

	%
Good idea	77
Poor idea	19
DK	4

Would you be willing to pay additional taxes to support such a program? (1976)

	%
Yes	51
No	21
DK	5

Discussing Child's Progress

In your opinion, should or should not parents be asked to meet with school personnel before each new school semester to examine the grades, test scores, and career goals for each child and to work out a program to be followed both in school and at home? (1980)

	%
Yes	84
No	11
DK	5

Have you attended any meeting since last September where the chief topic was how you, as a parent, could increase the interest of your child(ren) in his (their) school work, how and when to do homework, and other such matters that show what can be done at home to help the child in school? (1972)

	Public School Parents %	Private School Parents %
Yes	37	41
No	61	56
DK	2	3

Thinking about your eldest child, have you at any time since the beginning of the school year discussed your child's progress or problems with any of your child's teachers? (1977, 1981)

1977

The findings showed that 79% of all parents whose children were 12 years of age and under had talked to one or more of their child's teachers about his/her progress since the beginning of the school year. But only 55% of parents whose children were 13 years old and over had talked to any teacher.

1981

Results in the 1981 survey showed that 83% of the parents whose eldest child is 12 years of age or younger had discussed the child's progress or behavior with the child's teachers. For children 13 years of age and older the figure obtained in the 1981 study was 55%.

About how often since the beginning of the school year have you had discussions with your (eldest) child's teachers? (1977, 1981)

1977

In the case of parents whose eldest child was 12 years of age or younger, the median number of conferences was two.

The same figure — two — was the median for parent/teacher conferences for parents whose eldest child was 13 years of age or older.

1981

Number of Parent/Teacher Conferences Since the Beginning of School Year	Children 12 Years And Under %	Children 13 Years And Older %
One meeting	18	28
Two meetings	39	32
Three meetings	17	17
Four or five meetings	15	8
Six or more	10	14
DK	1	1

Thinking about the last time you spoke with your (eldest) child's teacher or teachers, did you feel that they were interested in discussing your child's work or behavior with you? (1981)

	%
Yes	80
No	7
DK	13

Parent Accountability

When some children do poorly in school, some people place the blame on children, some on the children's home life, some on the school, and some on the teachers. Of course, all of these things share the blame, but where would you place the chief blame? (1971, 1972)

	1971 %	1972 %*
Children	14	14
Home life	54	57
School	6	6
Teachers	8	12
DK	18	13

*Total more than 100% because of some multiple answers.

Participation

Since September, which of the following, if any, have you yourself done? (1983)

	National Totals %	No Children in School %	Public School Parents %	Nonpublic School Parents %
Received any newsletter, pamphlet, or any other material telling what the local public schools are doing	32	22	58	38
Attended a local public school athletic event	25	18	42	28
Attended a school play or concert in any local public school	24	16	42	36
Met with any teachers or administrators in the local public school about your own child	21	4	62	44
Attended a PTA meeting	14	4	36	46
Attended any meeting dealing with the local public school situation	10	7	18	13
Attended a school board meeting	8	4	16	24
Written any letter to the school board, newspaper, or any other organization about the local school situation	4	3	6	5
None of the above	43	56	14	22
DK	4	4	2	6

(Figures add to more than 100% because of multiple responses.)

Attendance at School Functions

Have you attended any lecture, any meeting, or any social occasion in any school building during the last year? (1969, 1979)

	1969 %	1979 %
Yes	37	33
No	59	64
DK	4	3

Have you *ever* attended a school board meeting? (1969)

	%
Yes	16
No	81
DK	3

PTA

Do you belong to the PTA or a similar group? (1969)

	Public School Parents %	Parochial School Parents %
Yes	52	65
No	48	35

If "no": Since you do have children in school, what are the reasons for not belonging to the PTA or a similar group? (1969)

	Public School Parents %	Parochial School Parents %
No time	22	11
Not interested	11	10
No PTA or similar group	9	10
New in this area	2	1
Health prevents attending	2	–
Miscellaneous	1	3
DK	2	–
	48*	35*

*Total equals percent who do not belong.

Do you attend [PTA] meetings regularly during the school year, or not? (1969) (Asked of those who said, "Belong to PTA.")

	Public School Parents %	Parochial School Parents %
Regularly	22	36
Not regularly	30	28
DK	–	1
	52*	65*

*Equals percent of those belonging to PTA.

"Will you please tell me why you do not regularly attend?" (1969) (Asked of those who said, "Do not attend regularly.")

	Public School Parents %	Parochial School Parents %
No time	20	18
Not interested	6	5
Health prevents attending	1	1
Miscellaneous	3	1
DK	1	3
	30*	28*

*Equals percent of those not regularly attending PTA.

Teachers and Teaching

Overall Professional Image

Would you like to have a child of yours take up teaching in the public schools as a career? (1969, 1972, 1980, 1981, 1983)

	1969 %	1972 %	1980 %	1981 %	1983 %
Yes	75	67	48	46	45
No	15	22	40	43	33
DK	10	11	12	11	22

How about a *daughter*. Would you like to have a daughter of yours take up teaching in the public schools as a career? (1981)

How about a *son*. Would you like to have a son of yours take up teaching in the public schools as a career? (1981)

	Daughter %	Son %
Yes	46	43
No	44	47
DK	10	10

Now I'd like your impressions about different professions and occupations — based on your personal experience, on what you've heard or read, or anything at all. To indicate your impression please use this scale, which goes from the lowest rating of zero to the highest rating of 10. [Respondents were shown a card with the scale printed on it.] First would you rate the following professions for the amount each contributes to the general good of society. The more you feel it contributes to the good of society, the higher the number you would pick — the less you feel it contributes, the lower the number. First, how would you rate ...? Now, for the amount of stress or pressure ...? Now, for the amount of prestige or status people in each profession have in this community? (1981)

Percent Receiving Highest Rating

	General Good of Society %	Stress or Pressure %	Prestige or Status %
Clergymen	46	26	42
Medical doctors	41	49	59
Public school teachers	29	43	19
Public school principals	28	42	25
Judges	23	36	48
Funeral directors	20	13	17
Bankers	14	22	35
Lawyers	12	21	31
Business executives	10	30	23
Local political officeholders	8	14	16
Realtors	7	10	6
Advertising practitioners	4	12	8

Image of Best Teachers

Looking back on your own school experience, did you find, in general, that the most effective teachers were under 40 years of age, or over 40 years of age? (1981)

	%
Under	32
Over	43
Same	21
DK	4

Perceived Difficulty in Obtaining Teachers

Do you think this local public school system has a hard time *getting* good teachers?
Do you think this local public school system has a hard time *keeping* good teachers? (1969)

	Getting %	Keeping %
Yes	52	48
No	32	35
DK	16	17

Do you think there are some teachers in the local public school system who should be dropped or fired? (1969)

	%
Yes	38
No	22
DK	40

Teacher Qualification and Accountability

Teachers now receive certificates to teach upon completion of their college coursework. Some people believe that teachers should be required to spend one year as interns in the schools at half pay before they are given a certificate to teach. Do you think this is a good idea or a poor idea? (1980)

	%
Good idea	56
Poor idea	36
DK	8

In addition to meeting college requirements for a teacher's certificate, should those who want to become teachers also be required to pass a state board examination to prove their knowledge in the subject(s) they will teach before they are hired? (1979, 1981)

	1979 %	1981 %
Yes	85	84
No	9	11
DK	6	5

After they are hired, do you think teachers should be tested every few years to see if they are keeping up to date with developments in their fields? (1979)

	%
Yes	85
No	10
DK	5

Would you favor or oppose a system that would hold teachers and administrators more accountable for the progress of students? (1970)

	%
Favor	67
Oppose	21
DK	12

Suppose you could choose your child's teachers. Assuming they all had about the same experience and training, what personal qualities would you look for? (1976, 1983)

1976
Rank Order
1. The ability to communicate, to understand, to relate
2. Ability to discipline, be firm and fair
3. The ability to inspire, motivate the child
4. High moral character
5. Love of children, concern for them
6. Dedication to teaching profession, enthusiasm
7. Friendly, good personality
8. Good personal appearance, cleanliness

1983
Rank Order
1. Ability to communicate, to understand, to relate
2. Patience
3. Ability to discipline, to be firm and fair
4. High moral character
5. Friendliness, good personality, sense of humor
6. Dedication to teaching profession, enthusiasm
7. Ability to inspire, motivate students
8. Intelligence
9. Caring about students

Tenure

Many states have "tenure" laws, which mean that a teacher cannot be fired except by some kind of court procedure. Are you for giving teachers tenure or are you against tenure? (1970)

	%
For	35
Against	53
DK	12

Do you happen to know what the word 'tenure' means as it applies to teachers' jobs? Just as you understand it, what does tenure mean? Do you favor or oppose tenure for teachers? (1977) (Based on those who knew what the term means.)

	%
Favor	40
Oppose	50
DK	10

Most public school teachers have tenure; that is, after a two- or three-year period, they receive what amounts to a lifetime contract. Do you approve or disapprove of this policy? (1972, 1974, 1981)

	1972 %	1974 %	1981 %
Approve	28	31	28
Disapprove	61	56	63
DK	11	13	9

If teachers must be laid off to save money in a school system, do you believe that those who are to be kept should be chosen on the basis of performance or on the basis of seniority? (1981)

	%
Performance	78
Seniority	17
DK	5

Teacher Pay

Do you think salaries in this community for teachers are too high, too low, or just about right? (1969, 1981, 1983)

	1969 %	1981 %	1983 %
Too high	2	10	8
Too low	33	29	35
About right	43	41	31
DK	22	20	26

(With DK group eliminated)	1969 %	1981 %	1983 %
Too high	3	13	11
Too low	42	36	47
About right	55	51	42

Are teachers in this community paid more money, or less money, than teachers in other comparable communities? (1969)

	%
More	12
Less	17
Same	34
DK	37

Should each teacher be paid on the basis of the quality of his work or should all teachers be paid on a standard scale basis? (1970, 1983)

	1970 %	1983 %
Quality of work	58	61
Standard scale	36	31
DK	6	8

Do you think teachers should be given automatic raises, or should raises be given to some and not to others? (1969)

	%
Automatic	44
Not automatic	45
DK	11

Today there is a shortage of teachers in science, math, technical subjects, and vocational subjects. If your local public schools needed teachers in these subjects, would you favor or oppose paying them higher wages than teachers of other subjects? (1983)

	%
Favor paying them higher wages	50
Oppose	35
DK	15

From what you know, are teachers in your community pretty well satisfied with their pay and working conditions or are they dissatisfied? (1969)

	%
Satisfied	35
Dissatisfied	35
DK	30

Teacher Organizations/Unions

How do you feel about teachers joining labor unions? Do you favor or oppose it? (1969)

	%
Favor	45
Oppose	40
DK	15

Most teachers in the nation now belong to unions or associations that bargain over salaries, working conditions, and the like. Has unionization, in your opinion, helped, hurt, or made no difference in the quality of public school education in the U.S.? (1976, 1981)

	1976 %	1981 %
Helped	22	18
Hurt	38	37
Made no difference	27	33
DK	13	12

In schools where there are teacher unions, should those teachers who do not belong to the union be required to pay union dues, since they share the benefits of union bargaining? (1980) (Asked of the public and of teachers)

	Public %	Teachers %
Yes, pay	47	33
No	44	64
DK	9	3

Have teacher organizations gained too much power over their own salaries and working conditions? (1970)

	%
Yes	26
No	53
DK	21

Some teacher groups want to extend their bargaining powers beyond pay and working conditions. They would like to have the right to negotiate about class size, the curriculum, and teaching methods. Would you favor or oppose giving them these added rights? (1976)

	%
Favor	52
Oppose	39
DK	9

Teacher Strikes

Should public school teachers be permitted to strike or not? (1969, 1975, 1980, 1981)

	1969 %	1975 %	1980 %	1981 %
Yes	37	45	40	37
No	59	48	52	56
DK	4	7	8	7

In case an agreement can not be reached between a teachers union (or association) and the school board, would you favor or oppose a plan that would require the dispute to be settled by the decision of an arbitrator or panel acceptable to both the union and school board? (1975, 1982)

	1975 %	1982 %
Favor	84	79
Oppose	7	7
DK	9	14

Burnout

Public school teachers are leaving the classroom in great numbers. Here are some reasons that are sometimes given. Which *three* of these do you think are the main reasons why teachers are leaving their jobs? (1982)

	%
Discipline problems in the schools	63
Low teacher salaries	52
Students are unmotivated/uninterested in school	37
Parents don't support teachers	37
Parents are not interested in children's progress	25
Lack of public financial support for education	24
Low standing of teaching as a profession	15
Difficulty of advancement	14
Outstanding teacher performance goes unrewarded	14
DK	4

Principals and Administrators

Principals as Management

Should principals be considered a part of management? (1975)

	%
Yes	80
No	11
DK	9

The law may require hiring as many women school principals as men. Which would you personally prefer for this job — a man or a woman? (1975)

	%
Prefer man	39
Prefer woman	7
No difference	52
DK	2

Accountability

Should school administrators be tested every few years to see if they are keeping up-to-date? (1979)

	%
Yes	85
No	10
DK	5

How do you feel about having guidance counselors in the public schools? Do you think they are worth the added cost? (1970)

	%
Yes	73
No	16
DK	11

In your opinion, should or should not the public schools add personnel to help students and recent graduates get jobs? (1980)

	%
Yes	64
No	30
DK	6

School Boards

Influence of Groups on Local Education

In your opinion, is there any group of people in this community that has more influence than it should have in the way schools are run? (If yes, Who is that?) (1978)

	%
Yes, too much	20
No	46
DK	34

No one group was named by more than a small minority. Oddly enough, the local school board was often named, underscoring the finding of another survey that many persons are unaware of the function of local school boards.

Politicians received some mention, as did blacks and the NAACP, the PTA, and "the wealthy." But on the whole the public seemed to feel in 1978 that no outside group was excessively powerful in influencing the schools.

Rating

Thinking about the school board in your school district, how much respect and confidence do you have in its ability to deal with school problems — a great deal of confidence, a fair amount, very little, or none? (1978)

	%
Great deal	18
Fair amount	43
Very little	16
None	6
DK	17

How good a job do you think the school board does? (1969)

	%
Excellent	25
Above average	16
Fair	21
Poor, terrible	7
DK	31

Now a question about the local school board. Does it work hard to improve the quality of education? (1969, 1972) Does it see that schools function efficiently and at the lowest costs? (1969) Is it politically motivated? (1969)

	Work Hard 1969 %	Work Hard 1972 %	Schools Function Efficiently 1969 %	Politically Motivated 1969 %
Yes	69	59	62	44
No	11	19	15	39
DK	20	22	23	17

Support for Increased Power for School Board

Local school policies are set, not only by the local school board, but also by the state government and the federal government. In the years ahead, would you like to see the local school board have greater responsibility in running the schools, or less, than they do today? (1976)

	%
Greater responsibility	67
Less responsibility	10
About the same	15
DK	8

Interested in Being a Member

If someone asked you to be a school board member, would you be interested? (1969)

	%
Yes	31
No	67
DK	2

Why do you say that? (1969)

Those who say "yes"	%
Interested in helping	27
Am qualified	4

Those who say "no"	%
Not qualified	31
Don't have time	15
Not interested	9
Have no children in school	9
Too much responsibility	6

Changes Would Seek

If you were to become a school board member, what changes in the schools would you favor? (1969)

	%
Curriculum, courses, course content	15
Professional staff	14
Buildings and facilities	11
Better discipline	9
Financial	4
Transportation	3
Segregation/integration	2
Miscellaneous	2
I'd make no changes	11
DK	44

College

Importance

How important is a college education today: ...very important, fairly important, or not too important? (1978, 1983)...extremely important, fairly important, not too important, or not important at all? (1974) (In 1974 this question was asked only of high school juniors and seniors.)

	1974 %	1978 %	1983 %
Very (extremely)	34	36	58
Fairly	51	46	31
Not too	10	16	8
Not at all	2	-	-
DK	1	2	3

Would you like to have your eldest child go on to college after graduating from high school? Why? (1982) (asked of parents only)

	Public School Parents %	Nonpublic School Parents %
Yes	87	84
No	5	6
DK	8	10

Reasons Offered	%*
More job opportunities/better income	48
Need more education today to cope with problems	27
Have a better life	20
College allows more time to mature	4
Miscellaneous	11

*Total equals more than 100% because of multiple answers.

Do you think he/she *will* go to college? (1982)

	Public School Parents %	Nonpublic School Parents %
Yes	57	67
No	19	15
DK	24	18

Who Bears the Cost

Some people say that the federal government should pay all of the cost of a college education. Others believe that most of the costs should continue to be paid, as now, by parents and students. Which would you favor? (1969)

	%
Federal government pays	16
Parents and students pay	70
Federal government and parents/students	7
Other methods	4
DK	3

Loans

The federal government now makes available at low interest rates loans to students who attend college. The administration in Washington now thinks the loans should go to students from low-income families only. Should these loans be available to all students or only to students from low-income families? (1981)

	%
Limit loans to students from low-income families	36
Do not limit	59
DK	5

Youth Unemployment Jobs

In your opinion, should or should not the public schools add personnel to help students and recent graduates get jobs? (1980)

	%
Yes	64
No	30
DK	6

In your opinion, are the opportunities for young people to obtain part-time jobs in this community good, only fair, or poor? (1978)

	%
Good	28
Only fair	39
Poor	25
DK	8

It has been suggested that the public schools be given the responsibility to set up special job training programs for young people, age 15 to 18, who are out of work and out of school. Would you favor or oppose such a plan? (1975)

	%
Favor	86
Oppose	11
DK	3

As you may know, the United States has a youth unemployment problem. It has been suggested that we develop a national youth service which would require every young man under the age of 20 who is unemployed, and not attending school or college, to take vocational or on-the-job training, or to perform public or military service until he reaches the age of 20. Would you approve or disapprove of such a national youth service plan for young men? Would you approve or disapprove of such a national youth service plan for young women? (1979)

	Young Men %	Young Women %
Approve	67	62
Disapprove	27	31
DK	6	7

Adult Education

Are you now taking, or have you ever taken, any courses in an adult education program? (1978, 1980)

	1978 %	1980 %
Yes	31	29
No	68	70
DK	1	1

Would you be interested next year in taking any special courses or training in any fields or in any subjects? (1978)

	%
Yes	41
No	54
DK	5

Preschool

Day-Care Centers

A proposal has been made to make child-care centers available for all preschool children as part of the public school system. This program would be supported by taxes. Would you favor or oppose such a program in your school district? (1976, 1981)

	1976 %	1981 %
Favor	46	46
Oppose	49	47
DK	5	7

Should the parents of preschool children participating in such a program be required to pay some of the costs for this day care? (1981)

	%
Parents should pay	83
Parents should not	10
DK	7

Do you think the school could help you in any way in preparing your child for school? (1979)

	Yes %	No %	DK %
Parents who presently have no children in school	53	34	13
Parents with one or more children in public school	37	53	10
Parents with one or more children in parochial school	40	40	20

National Commission on Excellence in Education

Have you heard or read anything about the recent report of the President's National Commission on Excellence in Education? (1983)

	%
Yes	28
No	68
DK	4

In general, do you agree or disagree with the report's conclusions? (1983) (Asked of informed group only)

	%
Agree	87
Disagree	8
DK	5

The Commission concluded that the quality of education in the U.S. public schools is only fair and not improving. Do you agree with this opinion or disagree? (1983) (Asked of uninformed group only)

	%
Agree	74
Disagree	13
DK	13

Would you be willing to pay more taxes to help raise the standard of education in the United States? (1983)

	National Totals %	No Children In School %	Public School Parents %	Nonpublic School Parents %
Yes	58	54	70	57
No	33	35	24	38
DK	9	11	6	5

Miscellaneous

Some girls get married before they are through high school. If they become pregnant, should they be permitted to attend? (1970)

	%
Yes	46
No	47
DK	7

If high school students can meet academic requirements in three years instead of four, should they, or should they not, be permitted to graduate early? (1977)

	%
Yes, they should	74
No, they should not	22
DK	4

Some children have such bad home conditions that they run away or are unable to function in the regular public school. Should live-in boarding schools be provided at public expense for these children? (1976)

	%
Yes	39
No	50
DK	11

Some students are not able to keep up with their classmates and therefore fail their work. Which of these two ways of dealing with this problem do you prefer? (1974)

	%
Promote them anyway	7
Hold them back	90
DK	3

Most people who have jobs today do not get home from work until 5:00 p.m. or later. In your opinion, should the schools arrange the afternoon school schedule so that children would get home at about the same time as their parents, or not? (1977)

	%
Yes	33
No	59
DK	8

Which one [of listed school goals] do you think is most neglected by parents today? (1976)

	%
High moral standards	32
Willingness to accept responsibility	30
Learning to think for oneself	14
Ability to get along with others	8
Eagerness to learn	5
Desire to excel	4
DK	7

And which one do you think is more neglected by schools? (1976)

	%
High moral standards	26
Learning to think for oneself	15
Eagerness to learn	13
Willingness to accept responsibility	12
Desire to excel	9
Ability to get along with others	8
DK	17

Is this child at the top of his/her class, above average, average, or below average in his/her grades? (1974) (Asked of parents who responded for their eldest child.)
Where do you stand academically in your class — near the top, above average, or below average? (1974) (Asked of high school juniors and seniors.)

	Parents of School Children %	High School Juniors & Seniors %
Near top	20	23
Above average	34	30
Average	40	45
Below average	4	2
DK	2	–

The number of one-parent families in the U.S. is growing each year due to the high divorce rate, and it is predicted that nearly half of the children born in 1980 will live, for a considerable period of time, with only one parent. Because of this, some people believe that the schools must find new ways to deal with the children from these broken homes. Of course, this will cost more money. Now, here are three proposals. For each one tell me whether you think is would be a good idea or a poor idea for the schools here. (1980)

		%
Proposal 1: Make school personnel available for evening counseling with single parents who are working if their children are having trouble at school.	Good idea Poor idea DK	86 10 4
Proposal 2: Give teachers training to help them deal with special problems of children from one-parent families.	Good idea Poor idea DK	83 12 5
Proposal 3: Provide activities so children can spend more time at school rather than going to an empty house.	Good idea Poor idea DK	76 18 6

Do the reports you receive on the progress of your [eldest] child in school provide you with the information you would like to have, or should the reports contain additional information that would be helpful? (1979)

	Public School Parents %	Parochial School Parents %
Satisfied	62	67
Dissatisfied	32	13
DK	6	20

Would you favor or oppose the idea of having your school board hire management experts to look into the costs of local schools to see if the educational goals could be achieved at less cost? (1971)

	%
Favor	54
Oppose	31
DK	15

Looking Ahead

As you look ahead to the year 2000 (that's 17 years from now), what do you think the schools will be doing then to education students? (1983)

Do you think that all students will have access to a computer and be trained in its use?

	%
Yes	86
No	6
DK	8

Do you think that more importance will be given to vocational training in high school?		%
	Yes	76
	No	11
	DK	13

Do you think that more attention will be given to teaching students how to think?		%
	Yes	70
	No	16
	DK	14

Do you think that what is now covered in the first two years of college will be covered before graduation from high school?		%
	Yes	65
	No	19
	DK	16

Do you think that more attention will be given to individual instruction?		%
	Yes	53
	No	32
	DK	15

Do you think children will start school at an earlier age — such as 3 or 4 years old?		%
	Yes	51
	No	37
	DK	12

Do you think that taxpayers will be willing to vote more favorably on bond issues and give more financial support to the schools?		%
	Yes	45
	No	36
	DK	19

Do you think that the school program will cover 12 months of the year — with less time for holidays?		%
	Yes	33
	No	53
	DK	14

1984 Gallup Poll of the Public's Attitudes Toward the Public Schools

Purpose of the Study

THIS SURVEY, which measures the attitudes of Americans toward their public schools, is the 16th annual survey in this series. Funding for this survey was provided by Phi Delta Kappa, Inc. Each year the poll attempts to deal with issues of greatest concern both to educators and to the public. New as well as trend questions are included in this and every survey.

To insure that the survey would embrace the most important issues in the field of education, Phi Delta Kappa organized a meeting of various leaders in the field of education to discuss their ideas, evaluate proposed questions, and suggest new questions for the survey.

We wish to thank all those who contributed their ideas to this survey.

Research Procedure

The Sample. The sample used in this survey embraced a total of 1,515 adults (18 years of age and older). It is described as a modified probability sample of the United States. Personal, in-home interviewing was conducted in all areas of the U.S. and in all types of communities. A description of the sample can be obtained from Phi Delta Kappa.

Time of Interviewing. The fieldwork for this study was carried out during the period of 18-27 May 1984.

The Report. In the tables that follow, the heading "Nonpublic School Parents" includes parents of students who attend parochial schools and parents of students who attend private or independent schools.

Due allowance must be made for statistical variation, especially in the case of findings for small groups in which relatively few respondents were interviewed, e.g., nonpublic school parents.

The findings of this report apply only to the U.S. as a whole and not to individual communities. Local surveys, using the same questions, can be conducted to determine how local areas compare with national norms.

Summary of Findings

Americans are more favorably disposed toward the public schools today than at any time in the last decade. In this year's survey, more Americans (42%) grade their local schools A or B for their performance than at any time since 1976 — with an 11-point increase just since last year. Virtually the same dramatic increase occurs among the parents of public school children — with a 10% rise since last year in the percentage giving the local schools an A or B rating.

Americans have also become significantly more favorably disposed toward public school teachers and administrators. In 1981, 39% gave teachers a grade of A or B, whereas today the figure is 50%. Moreover, the A or B grades given to principals and administrators have risen from 36% to 47% during this same three-year period.

A final indicator that reveals an increase in favorable feelings toward the schools is the public's increased willingness to pay the price for public education. The percentage of Americans who say that they would be willing to pay more taxes for education has risen from 30% to 41%.

Americans continue to feel that public education contributes more to national strength than either industrial might or military power. More than eight in 10 say that developing the best educational system in the world will be "very important" in determining America's future strength, compared to 70% who favor developing the best industrial production system and only 45% who favor developing the strongest military force.

The American public is divided in its support for the various recommendations proposed in the recently published reports concerning U.S. education. The public strongly favors 1) increasing the amount of schoolwork and homework in both elementary and high school, 2) basing all grade promotions on examinations, and 3) employing nationally standardized tests for high school diplomas. Support for each of these proposals has increased in recent years.

Americans also support, by wide margins, the ideas of career ladders for teachers and state board teacher examinations in every subject. To a lesser degree, the public feels that salaries for teachers are too low; Americans support higher pay for teachers where shortages exist, including mathematics, science, technical subjects, vocational training, and other critical areas.

Americans give top priority to the traditional "basics" — math and English — as has been the case since these annual surveys were initiated; there is virtually unanimous agreement that these courses should be required of all high school students — both college-bound and non-college-bound. Several of the so-called "new basics" (i.e., science and computer science) are considered less important, though both have recorded gains since 1981, particularly computer science. Similarly, vocational training as a requirement for non-college-bound students has registered substantial gains. The issue of foreign language as a requirement for college-bound students, however, has made little progress in recent years. The number of Americans who feel that extracurricular activities are very important to a young person's education has dropped from 45% in 1978 to 31% today.

The public appears to be unwilling to make some of the necessary sacrifices or commitments to help implement some of the recommendations of the school reform reports. Americans are opposed to extended school years or longer school days, which would provide the time for additional schooling. (Support for both ideas has increased somewhat in the last few years, however.) Furthermore, nonparents as well as parents oppose by a 2-1 margin the tougher college admission standards that are the logical extension of stricter standards at the elementary and high school levels.

Although teachers oppose merit pay as a means of rewarding outstanding teaching performance by a margin of roughly 2-1, the public (including parents and nonparents) *favors* the idea by about 3-1. Among the half of the population who are familiar with merit pay, support rises to roughly 4-1.

Approximately seven Americans in 10 favor school prayer — one of the most controversial issues facing the public schools today. At the same time, though the survey question omitted the word *voluntary*, a separate Gallup Poll measuring support for *voluntary* prayer shows some decline in support for the proposal.

Although Americans have tended to favor Ronald Reagan as President over Walter Mondale, they feel that Mondale would be more likely than Reagan — by 42% to 34% — to improve the quality of education. In addition, 66% of Americans say that they would be more likely to vote for a candidate who favored increased federal spending for education; only 22% say that they would be less likely to vote for such a candidate.

The American public continues to regard discipline as the most important problem facing the public schools; about one-fourth of Americans cite discipline as the predominant problem, as they have done for more than a decade. Our analysis indicates that this is probably an outcome of the public's exaggerated perceptions of specific disciplinary problems that occur in the schools — especially when these findings are compared to the testimony of those most likely to know the actual situation, the teachers. Half of the American public feels that drugs are used in the local schools "most of the time" or "fairly often." About one-third of the public feels that theft of money or personal property, drinking of alcoholic beverages, theft of school property, and carrying of knives or other weapons occur "most of the time" or "fairly often."

MONITORING MEASURES

Education in America's Future

The American public is strongly in favor of developing the best educational system in the world. In fact, U.S. citizens believe — as they did in 1982, when this question was first asked — that education will be more important in determining America's place in the world 25 years from now than our industrial system or our military might.

The question:

In determining America's strength in the future — say, 25 years from now — how important do you feel each of the following factors will be — very important, fairly important, not too important, or not at all important?

	Very Important %	Fairly Important %	Not Too Important %	Not At All Important %	Don't Know %
Developing the best educational system in the world	82	13	2	1	2
Developing the most efficient industrial production system in the world	70	23	3	1	3
Building the strongest military force in the world	45	36	13	3	3

Those responding very important	1984 %	1982 %
Developing the best educational system in the world	82	84
Developing the most efficient industrial production system in the world	70	66
Building the strongest military force in the world	45	47

1984 Rating of the Public Schools

The downward trend in the public's rating of the public schools recorded in these surveys during the last decade has ended. This year, 42% of those interviewed gave an A or B rating to the public schools in their communities, up sharply from 31% in 1983. Not since 1976 have these ratings been so high.

The higher rating given the schools this year may have resulted from two developments. First, the reports of the national commissions that have examined schooling in America have caused widespread debate concerning the quality of public education. Citizens have taken a closer look at their own schools and presumably found them better than they had previously believed. Also, many schools have heeded the criticisms made in the reports and have instituted reforms in their educational programs.

It is noteworthy that parents also give their schools a higher rating this year: 52% A or B, as opposed to 42% in 1983.

The question:

Students are often given the grades A,B,C,D, and FAIL to denote the quality of their work. Suppose the *public* schools themselves, in this community, were graded in the same way. What grade would you give the public schools here — A,B,C,D, or FAIL?

	National Totals %	No Children In School %	Public School Parents %	Nonpublic School Parents %
A rating	10	8	15	4
B rating	32	31	37	33
C rating	35	35	32	42
D rating	11	10	12	16
FAIL	4	5	3	4
Don't know	8	11	1	1

Ratings Given The Local Public Schools	1984 %	1983 %	1982 %	1981 %	1980 %	1979 %	1978 %	1977 %	1976 %
A rating	10	6	8	9	10	8	9	11	13
B rating	32	25	29	27	25	26	27	26	29
C rating	35	32	33	34	29	30	30	28	28
D rating	11	13	14	13	12	11	11	11	10
FAIL	4	7	5	7	6	7	8	5	6
Don't know	8	17	11	10	18	18	15	19	14

Further breakdowns:

	A %	B %	C %	D %	FAIL %	Don't Know %
NATIONAL TOTALS	10	32	35	11	4	8
Sex						
Men	9	33	34	11	5	8
Women	10	32	36	11	3	8
Race						
White	10	33	34	11	4	8
Nonwhite	11	26	38	10	6	9
Age						
18 - 29 years	7	27	43	13	5	5
30 - 49 years	10	33	37	11	4	5
50 and over	11	35	27	9	5	13
Community Size						
1 million and over	9	29	37	12	5	8
500,000 - 999,999	5	34	37	16	3	5
50,000 - 499,999	9	29	34	14	6	8
2,500 - 49,999	8	43	31	6	3	9
Under 2,500	13	34	31	7	5	10
Central city	6	27	38	15	7	7
Education						
Grade school	14	27	29	8	5	17
High school	8	33	35	12	5	7
College	10	33	36	12	3	6
Region						
East	9	30	37	13	5	6
Midwest	13	37	30	8	4	8
South	8	35	33	10	5	9
West	9	25	40	14	4	8

Rating of Public Schools Nationally

This year's survey also shows an upward trend in the public's rating of the public schools nationally. But, as the ratings indicate, respondents continue to give schools in their own communities higher marks than they do the public schools nationally.

The question:

How about the public schools in the nation as a whole? What grade would you give the public schools nationally — A, B, C, D, or FAIL?

	National Totals %	No Children In School %	Public School Parents %	Nonpublic School Parents %
A rating	2	2	3	4
B rating	23	24	21	19
C rating	49	47	52	52
D rating	11	10	13	15
FAIL	4	4	2	4
Don't know	11	13	9	6

Public Schools in the Nation

	1984 %	1983 %	1982 %	1981 %
A rating	2	2	2	2
B rating	23	17	20	18
C rating	49	38	44	43
D rating	11	16	15	15
FAIL	4	6	4	6
Don't know	11	21	15	16

Rating of Teachers in the Local Public Schools

The 1984 survey indicates that the public has increasing respect for the teachers in the local schools. Half of all respondents give teachers an A or B rating. This is considerably higher than the rating given to teachers in the 1981 survey.

The highest ratings go to teachers in small communities — those with a population under 2,500. The lowest ratings go to teachers in the central cities, where the teaching problems are greatest.

Respondents living in the Midwest give their teachers a slightly higher rating than do citizens living in other areas of the U.S.

The question:

Now, what grade would you give the teachers in the public schools in this community?

	National Totals %	No Children In School %	Public School Parents %	Nonpublic School Parents %
A rating	13	13	15	6
B rating	37	35	43	34
C rating	31	31	29	42
D rating	7	6	8	9
FAIL	3	3	3	1
Don't know	9	12	2	8

	1984 %	1981 %
NATIONAL TOTALS		
A rating	13	11
B rating	37	28
C rating	31	31
D rating	7	9
FAIL	3	6
Don't know	9	15

Further breakdowns:

	A %	B %	C %	D %	FAIL %	Don't Know %
NATIONAL TOTALS	13	37	31	7	3	9
Sex						
Men	12	38	31	7	3	9
Women	14	37	31	6	3	9
Race						
White	13	38	30	7	3	9
Nonwhite	13	33	33	6	3	12
Age						
18 - 29 years	11	33	38	7	4	7
30 - 49 years	13	39	32	8	2	6
50 and over	15	39	24	6	2	14
Community Size						
1 million and over	12	35	35	6	3	9
500,000 - 999,999	17	38	25	10	2	8
50,000 - 499,999	9	37	33	8	2	11
2,500 - 49,999	15	39	27	5	4	10
Under 2,500	17	41	19	5	5	13
Central city	9	34	36	9	3	9
Education						
Grade school	13	36	21	7	4	19
High school	13	34	34	7	4	8
College	13	42	29	7	1	8
Region						
East	11	40	31	6	5	7
Midwest	16	41	27	5	2	9
South	13	34	33	8	2	10
West	11	34	33	8	3	11

Rating of Principals and Administrators In the Local Public Schools

The ratings given to school principals and other administrators are somewhat similar to those given to teachers. As in the case of teachers, the ratings in the 1984 survey are appreciably higher than those in the 1981 survey.

The question:

Now, what grade would you give the principals and administrators in the local public schools in this community?

	National Totals %	No Children In School %	Public School Parents %	Nonpublic School Parents %
A rating	13	12	18	5
B rating	34	32	36	42
C rating	29	30	27	27
D rating	8	7	10	13
FAIL	5	5	5	6
Don't know	11	14	4	7

NATIONAL TOTALS	1984 %	1981 %
A rating	13	10
B rating	34	26
C rating	29	28
D rating	8	12
FAIL	5	9
Don't know	11	15

Rating of the School Board In This Community

This year's survey, for the first time, rates school boards on the same scale as that employed to rate the schools, teachers, administrators, and parents.

Understandably, those who have little contact with the public schools say that they do not know enough about their local school boards to assign a rating. Parents with children now enrolled in either public or nonpublic schools rate school boards only slightly lower than they rate the schools themselves. The highest rating is given by respondents who have children now enrolled in the public schools.

The question:

Now, what grade would you give the school board in this community?

	National Totals %	No Children In School %	Public School Parents %	Nonpublic School Parents %
A rating	9	9	11	5
B rating	32	31	33	33
C rating	29	27	29	39
D rating	11	10	14	14
FAIL	6	6	8	5
Don't know	13	17	5	4

Rating Given to Parents of Students In the Public Schools

Parents of children now attending the public schools are not too pleased with the way public school parents are bringing up their children. In fact, they give themselves, collectively, lower marks for the way they are doing their job than they give teachers and school administrators.

Only 39% give parents a grade of A or B. This contrasts with a figure of 58% for teachers and 54% for principals and other school administrators.

Parents with children attending nonpublic schools give parents of public school students even lower grades. Only 29% give public school parents an A or B rating; 26% give them a D or FAIL rating.

The question:

Now, what grade would you give the parents of students in the local public schools for bringing up their children?

	National Totals %	No Children In School %	Public School Parents %	Nonpublic School Parents %
A rating	7	6	9	6
B rating	26	25	30	23
C rating	36	36	35	40
D rating	16	15	19	16
FAIL	6	6	5	10
Don't know	9	12	2	5

NATIONAL TOTALS	1984 %	1981* %
A rating	7	5
B rating	26	24
C rating	36	36
D rating	16	16
FAIL	6	11
Don't know	9	8

*The wording of the question in the 1981 survey was: "What grade would you give parents in this community for the job they are doing in raising their children to be self-disciplined and responsible young people — A,B,C,D, or FAIL?"

Tax Increases to Support The Public Schools

Since the spring of 1983, when the National Commission on Excellence in Education presented its report, a slight increase has been registered in the percentage of citizens who favor a tax increase in situations where the schools say that they need much more money.

The percentage of public school parents who favor such a tax increase has risen from 48% in 1983 to 54% today, while the percentage of those opposed has dropped from 45% to 38%.

Those respondents who have attended college are most in favor of tax increases. When sections of the U.S. are compared, residents of the western states are found to be most in favor of raising taxes to help the schools.

The question:

Suppose the local public schools said they needed much more money. As you feel at this time, would you vote to raise taxes for this purpose, or would you vote against raising taxes for this purpose?

	National Totals %	No Children In School %	Public School Parents %	Nonpublic School Parents %
For raise in taxes	41	37	54	42
Against raise in taxes	47	50	38	51
Don't know	12	13	8	7

Financial Support of the Public Schools

NATIONAL TOTALS	Favor Raising Taxes %	Opposed to Raising Taxes %	Don't Know %
1984 survey	41	47	12
1983 survey	39	52	9
1981 survey	30	60	10
1972 survey	36	56	8
1971 survey	40	52	8
1970 survey	37	56	7
1969 survey	45	49	6

CURRENT EDUCATION ISSUES

Presidential Candidate Perceived to Support Education More

At the time interviewing was conducted for this survey, Ronald Reagan held a wide lead in a Presidential trial heat against Walter Mondale (54% to 39%).

Despite this apparent preference for President Reagan, when the public was asked which candidate, Reagan or Mondale, would be more likely to improve the quality of education in the U.S., Mondale was named by a larger percentage than the President — 42% to 34%. Nearly a quarter of the public registered no opinion.

The question:

Which Presidential candidate do you feel would be more likely, as President, to improve the quality of public education in the U.S. — Ronald Reagan or Walter Mondale?

	National Totals %
Walter Mondale	42
Ronald Reagan	34
No opinion	24

Likelihood of Voting for Candidate Supporting Increased Spending for Education

Another measure of the public's willingness to spend more on education is elicited by a question asking whether respondents would be more likely to vote for a Presidential candidate who favored increased spending for education or less likely to vote for such a candidate.

Two-thirds of Americans (66%) would be more likely to vote for the candidate supporting increased spending. Only a third as many (22%) say that they would be less likely to vote for this candidate.

The question:

Would you be more likely or less likely to vote for a candidate who says he would increase federal spending for education?

	National Totals %
More likely	66
Less likely	22
Don't know	12

Increasing the Length of The School Year

Public sentiment in favor of increasing the length of the school year by one month is growing. In the 1982 survey a total of 37% approved of this plan. In 1983 approval reached 40%, and in the present survey the comparable figure is 44%. However, 50% in this year's survey still oppose this plan.

Those who are most in favor of a longer school year are residents of the cities with populations over one million. Most opposed are people living in smaller cities and in towns of 2,500 and under.

Those who have attended college favor a longer school year by a margin of 51% to 45%. Residents of the western states also approve a longer school year by a margin of 59% to 35%.

The question:

In some nations, students attend school as many as 240 days a year as compared to 180 days in the U.S. How do you feel about extending the public school year in this community by 30 days, making the school year about 210 days or 10 months long? Do you favor or oppose this idea?

	National Totals %	No Children In School %	Public School Parents %	Nonpublic School Parents %
Favor	44	44	45	46
Oppose	50	49	52	46
No opinion	6	7	3	8

NATIONAL TOTALS	1984 %	1983 %	1982 %
Favor	44	40	37
Oppose	50	49	53
No opinion	6	11	10

Further breakdowns:

	Favor %	Oppose %	No Opinion %
NATIONAL TOTALS	44	50	6
Sex			
Men	45	49	6
Women	42	51	7
Race			
White	44	50	6
Nonwhite	46	48	6
Age			
18 - 29 years	38	58	4
30 - 49 years	47	48	5
50 and over	45	46	9
Community Size			
1 million and over	52	42	6
500,000 - 999,999	48	49	3
50,000 - 499,999	42	50	8
2,500 - 49,999	39	56	5
Under 2,500	41	54	5
Central city	52	42	6
Education			
Grade school	34	53	13
High school	41	53	6
College	51	45	4
Region			
East	45	49	6
Midwest	37	55	8
South	39	55	6
West	59	35	6

Extending the School Day by One Hour

Although this year's survey findings indicate that the public is slightly more in favor of increasing the length of the school day by one hour than in 1982, a majority remain opposed.

Residents of the western states and the largest cities most strongly favor the longer school day. Residents of the Midwest are the most opposed.

The question:

How do you feel about extending the school day in the schools in this community by one hour? Do you favor or oppose this idea?

	National Totals %	No Children In School %	Public School Parents %	Nonpublic School Parents %
Favor	42	42	41	38
Oppose	52	51	56	58
No opinion	6	7	3	4

	1984 %	1983 %	1982 %
NATIONAL TOTALS			
Favor	42	41	37
Oppose	52	48	55
No opinion	6	11	8

Further breakdowns:

	Favor %	Oppose %	No Opinion %
NATIONAL TOTALS	42	52	6
Sex			
Men	42	52	6
Women	41	53	6
Race			
White	42	53	5
Nonwhite	40	52	8
Age			
18 - 29 years	32	65	3
30 - 49 years	43	52	5
50 and over	48	44	8
Community Size			
1 million and over	49	45	6
500,000 - 999,999	34	59	7
50,000 - 499,999	37	57	6
2,500 - 49,999	39	55	6
Under 2,500	46	48	6
Central city	45	48	7
Education			
Grade school	42	44	14
High school	40	55	5
College	45	51	4
Region			
East	46	49	5
Midwest	34	60	6
South	37	57	6
West	53	42	5

Amount of Schoolwork Required of Elementary and High School Students

All segments of the U.S. population agree that students in elementary schools and high schools are not made to work hard enough in school or on homework. This opinion has remained fairly constant in three surveys, the first in 1975.

Only 5% of those interviewed in this year's survey think that students are made to work too hard in elementary school, and only 4% think students in high school are made to work too hard. By contrast, 59% say that students are not required to work hard enough in elementary school, and 67% say that they are not required to work hard enough in high school.

Perhaps the best judges of whether students are being given enough schoolwork to do in school and at home are the parents of these students. Parents agree that their children are not being required to work hard enough. Only 7% of parents with children now enrolled in the public schools say that children in elementary school are required to work too hard; 54% say that they are not required to work hard enough. In the case of high school students, 5% of parents with children enrolled in public schools say that children are required to work too hard; 62% say that they are not required to work hard enough.

The question:

In general, do you think *elementary* schoolchildren in the public schools here are made to work too hard in school and on homework or not hard enough?

	National Totals %	No Children In School %	Public School Parents %	Nonpublic School Parents %
Too hard	5	5	7	4
Not hard enough	59	60	54	56
About right amount	24	20	34	30
Don't know	12	15	5	10

	1984 %	1983 %	1975 %
NATIONAL TOTALS			
Too hard	5	4	5
Not hard enough	59	61	49
About right amount	24	19	28
Don't know	12	16	18

The question:

What about students in the public *high schools* here — in general, are they required to work too hard or not hard enough?

	National Totals %	No Children In School %	Public School Parents %	Nonpublic School Parents %
Too hard	4	4	5	–
Not hard enough	67	69	62	69
About right amount	18	15	25	22
Don't know	11	12	8	9

	1984 %	1983 %	1975 %
NATIONAL TOTALS			
Too hard	4	3	3
Not hard enough	67	65	54
About right amount	18	12	22
Don't know	11	20	21

Subjects the Public Would Require

Mathematics and English head the list of subjects the public would require of high school students who plan to attend college; mathematics was mentioned by 96% of respondents, and English was mentioned by 94%.

In addition, a large majority would require history/U.S. government and science. Slightly fewer, but still a majority, would require courses in business, foreign language, and health education.

For *non*-college-bound students, the public would also require math and English and by virtually the same percentages as for those planning to go to college. Somewhat fewer respondents feel that history and science should be required of non-college-bound students, and far fewer favor a foreign language requirement.

Not surprisingly, a much larger percentage of Americans feel that vocational training should be required for non-college-bound students than for those planning to go to college. Similarly, business as a required course is favored by a slightly larger percentage for non-college-bound students.

Support for computer science as a required course — for both college- and non-college-bound students — has dramatically increased from 43% to 68% in just three years. Although support for a science requirement for non-college-bound students has risen only marginally, support for a science requirement for those planning to go to college has risen from 76% to 84% since 1981. On the other hand, support for a foreign language for college-bound students has made little progress in the past three years.

The questions:

> Would you look over this card, which lists high school subjects. If you were the one to decide, what subjects would you require every public high school student who *plans to go on to college* to take?
> What about those public high school students who do *not plan to go to college* when they graduate? Which courses would you require them to take?

Should Be Required

	For Those Planning To Go to College %	For Those Not Planning to Go To College %
Mathematics	96	92
English	94	90
History/U.S. government	84	71
Science	84	61
Business	68	76
Foreign language	57	19
Health education	52	50
Physical education	43	44
Vocational training	37	83
Art	24	18
Music	22	18

Should Be Required

	For Those Planning To Go to College			For Those Not Planning to Go To College		
	1984 %	1983 %	1981 %	1984 %	1983 %	1981 %
Mathematics	96	92	94	92	87	91
English	94	88	91	90	83	89
History/U.S. government	84	78	83	71	63	71
Science	84	76	76	61	53	58
Business	68	55	60	76	65	75
Foreign language	57	50	54	19	19	21
Health education	52	43	47	50	42	46
Physical education	43	41	44	44	40	43
Vocational training	37	32	34	83	74	64
Art	24	19	28	18	16	20
Music	22	18	26	18	16	20

Special Areas of Instruction That Should Be Required

The public would like the public schools to provide instruction in many aspects of modern life, in addition to the subjects traditionally included in the school curriculum. Heading the list of these special areas of instruction is drug abuse, followed by alcohol abuse. Large majorities of the population would also require instruction in such areas as driver education, computer training, race relations, and the dangers of nuclear waste.

The question:

> In addition to regular courses, high schools offer instruction in other areas. As I read off these areas, one at a time, would you tell me whether you feel this instruction should be required or should not be required for all high school students.

	Should Be Required %	Should Not Be Required %	No Opinion %
Drug abuse	82	15	3
Alcohol abuse	79	18	3
Driver education	73	25	2
Computer training	68	28	4
Race relations	65	29	6
Dangers of nuclear waste	61	34	5
Communism/socialism	57	37	6
Parenting/parent training	55	39	6
Dangers of nuclear war	51	43	6

Should Be Required

	1984 %	1983 %	1981 %
Drug abuse	82	81	82
Alcohol abuse	79	76	78
Driver education	73	72	71
Computer training	68	72	43
Race relations*	65	56	–
Dangers of nuclear waste*	61	56	–
Communism/socialism*	57	51	–
Parenting/parent training	55	58	64
Dangers of nuclear war*	51	46	–

*These topics were not included in the 1981 survey.

Importance of Extracurricular Activities

About three-quarters of the U.S. public (77%) feel that extracurricular activities are either "very important" or "fairly important" to a young person's education. At the same time, however, there has been a decline in the percentage of those who say that extracurricular activities are "very important" — from 45% in 1978 to 31% in 1984. During this same period there has been an increase in the percentage of the public who say that extracurricular activities are "not too important" — from 9% to 18%. This decrease in support may reflect, to some extent, the heavy emphasis placed on the academic curriculum by the various national reports on the state of education.

Better-educated Americans are more inclined to feel that extracurricular activities are important. A total of 84% of those who have attended college say that these activities are "very important" or "fairly important," while only 68% of those whose education ended with grade school regard such activities as important.

The question:

I'd like your opinion about extracurricular activities such as the school band, dramatics, sports, and the school paper. How important are these to a young person's education — very important, fairly important, not too important, or not at all important?

	National Totals %	No Children In School %	Public School Parents %	Nonpublic School Parents %
Very important	31	31	32	30
Fairly important	46	45	48	52
Not too important	18	18	16	14
Not at all important	4	4	3	3
No opinion	1	2	1	1

NATIONAL TOTALS	1984 %	1978 %
Very important	31	45
Fairly important	46	40
Not too important	18	9
Not at all important	4	4
No opinion	1	2

National Test for Graduation

The American public shows remarkable unanimity in favoring a standard nationwide test for graduation from high school. Only in communities under 2,500 is sentiment fairly closely divided on this proposal.

This question was first asked of a national cross section of adults in 1958, and the idea was favored at that time by a margin of 50% to 39%. When the same question was asked in 1981, 69% favored the proposal, 26% opposed it, and 5% had no opinion. Roughly the same results were found in this year's survey: 65% in favor, 29% opposed, and 6% with no opinion.

Many nations require students to pass standard examinations for graduation; in the United States, however, because of varying local conditions, such a plan has never been adopted. Nevertheless, the public appears to see merit in such a policy.

The question:

Should all high school students in the United States be required to pass a standard nationwide examination in order to get a high school diploma?

	National Totals %	No Children In School %	Public School Parents %	Nonpublic School Parents %
Yes	65	65	65	59
No	29	29	29	35
No opinion	6	6	6	6

NATIONAL TOTALS	1984 %	1981 %	1976 %	1958 %
Yes	65	69	65	50
No	29	26	31	39
No opinion	6	5	4	11

Raising College Entrance Requirements

Many educators have argued that raising the entrance requirements of colleges and universities would be an effective way of inducing the public schools to raise their standards. However, this proposal fails to win the approval of the public.

Analysis of the opinions of various groups in the population reveals that all major groups oppose this suggestion, especially those most concerned: parents of children now attending elementary or high school. Even those who have attended college vote against the idea.

The question:

Do you feel that four-year colleges and universities should raise their entrance requirements or not?

	National Totals %	No Children In School %	Public School Parents %	Nonpublic School Parents %
Yes	27	28	24	21
No	59	57	64	61
No opinion	14	15	12	18

State Board Examinations for Teachers

Survey findings reveal widespread agreement that prospective teachers should be required to pass state board examinations to prove their knowledge in the subjects they plan to teach.

More than eight in every 10 respondents have favored this policy in the three surveys in which this same question has been asked: 1979, 1981, and 1984.

The question:

In addition to meeting college requirements for a teacher's certificate, should those who want to become teachers also be required to pass a state board examination to prove their knowledge in the subjects they will teach before they are hired?

	National Totals %	No Children In School %	Public School Parents %	Nonpublic School Parents %
Yes	89	89	89	92
No	7	7	8	7
No opinion	4	4	3	1

NATIONAL TOTALS	1984 %	1981 %	1979 %
Yes	89	84	85
No	7	11	9
No opinion	4	5	6

Career Ladder for Teachers

The proposal to adopt a career ladder for public school teachers that is grounded in classroom effectiveness, with accompanying salary increases, is favored by a substantial majority (75%) of the public. In fact, by approximately the same percentages, all segments of the population agree that this is a good plan.

The question:

It has been suggested that public schools adopt a career ladder for teachers, based primarily upon demonstrated effectiveness in the classroom, with salaries increasing accordingly. Would you approve or disapprove if such a plan were adopted by the public schools in this community?

	National Totals %	No Children In School %	Public School Parents %	Nonpublic School Parents %
Approve	75	74	77	79
Disapprove	16	16	16	16
No opinion	9	10	7	5

Teachers' Salaries in This Community

The American public tends to feel that teachers' salaries are too low. Interestingly, this view is held by those who do not have children enrolled in the public schools, as well as by those who do.

On the other hand, those who have no children in the local schools are more likely to vote against tax increases and bond issues for the schools than those who have children enrolled.

During the last 15 years, attitudes concerning teachers' salaries have shown little change. The weight of opinion throughout this period has been that salaries are too low. This opinion is particularly prevalent among more highly educated citizens and among those who live in the southern states, where teacher salaries tend to be lowest.

The question:

Do you think salaries in this community for teachers are too high, too low, or just about right?

	National Totals %	No Children In School %	Public School Parents %	Nonpublic School Parents %
Too high	7	6	8	7
Too low	37	37	38	33
Just about right	41	40	41	47
No opinion	15	17	13	13

NATIONAL TOTALS	1984 %	1983 %	1981 %	1969 %
Too high	7	8	10	2
Too low	37	35	29	33
About right	41	31	41	43
No opinion	15	26	20	22

NATIONAL TOTALS (with "no opinion" group eliminated)	1984 %	1983 %	1981 %	1969 %
Too high	8	11	13	3
Too low	44	47	36	42
About right	48	42	51	55

Paying Math and Science Teachers More

Slightly more respondents in this year's survey favor than oppose paying higher wages to teachers of science, math, and technical and vocational subjects because of the shortage that now exists in these subject areas. However, only in the largest cities does the percentage reach 50% or higher.

When the same question was asked in 1983, national totals were 50% in favor, 35% opposed, and 15% don't know.

The question:

Today there is a shortage of teachers in science, math, technical subjects, and vocational subjects. If your local schools needed teachers in these subjects, would you favor or oppose paying them higher wages than teachers of other subjects?

	National Totals %	No Children In School %	Public School Parents %	Nonpublic School Parents %
Favor	48	46	52	56
Oppose	43	43	42	37
No opinion	9	11	6	7

NATIONAL TOTALS	1984 %	1981 %
Favor	48	50
Oppose	43	35
No opinion	9	15

Attitudes Toward Merit Pay Programs

Although the issue of merit pay for teachers seems to have provoked a great deal of discussion recently, when this survey was conducted only half of those interviewed said that they had heard or read anything about such programs.

When those who said that they were aware of merit pay proposals were asked whether they generally favored or opposed the idea, three-fourths (76%) said that they approved of it, 19% were opposed, and 5% had no opinion. For the total sample, the percentage who approve of the idea of merit pay is 65%, with 22% opposed and 13% having no opinion.

In 1970 and again in 1983 a merit pay question was asked in this form: "Should each teacher be paid on the basis of the quality of his or her work, or should all teachers be paid on a standard-scale basis?" In 1970, 58% said that teachers should be paid according to "quality of work," 36% on a "standard scale," and 6% said "don't know." Comparable figures for 1983 were 61%, 31%, and 8%.

The question:

Some states have recently adopted merit pay programs which would provide additional pay for outstanding teacher performance. Have you heard or read anything about these programs?

	National Totals %	No Children In School %	Public School Parents %	Nonpublic School Parents %
Yes	51	50	55	56
No	45	46	42	42
Don't know	4	4	3	2

The question:

How do you, yourself, feel about the idea of merit pay for teachers? In general, do you favor or oppose it?

Total Sample	National Totals %	No Children In School %	Public School Parents %	Nonpublic School Parents %
Favor	65	63	69	75
Oppose	22	23	20	14
No opinion	13	14	11	11

Those Who Have Heard or Read About Merit Pay for Teachers	National Totals %	No Children In School %	Public School Parents %	Nonpublic School Parents %
Favor	76	75	77	81
Oppose	19	20	19	10
No opinion	5	5	4	9

Criteria to Be Used in Awarding Merit Pay

One of the greatest hurdles facing merit pay is the difficulty of agreeing on the criteria to be used in deciding which teachers should receive extra pay. A list of possible criteria was compiled. To determine which criteria are most acceptable to the public, respondents were asked in the case of each criterion whether they thought it should or should not be used to decide which teachers should be given additional pay.

Seven criteria are listed below in order of their acceptability to the public. Improvement achieved by students as measured by standardized tests is rated highest. Virtually the same rating is given to the evaluations of administrators. Gaining almost the same high approval is an advanced degree, such as the master's or Ph.D. Evaluation by other teachers, length of teaching experience, students' evaluations, and parents' opinions have support, but not majority support.

The question:

This card lists possible criteria for giving additional pay to teachers for special merit. As I read off each one by letter, please tell me if you think it should or should not be used to determine which teachers should receive merit pay.

	Should Be Criterion %	Should Not Be Criterion %	No Opinion %
Academic achievement or improvement of students (as measured by standardized tests)	68	25	7
Administrators' evaluations	67	26	7
An advanced degree, such as a master's or Ph.D.	66	27	7
Evaluation by other teachers in the system	48	42	10
Length of teaching experience	48	47	5
Students' evaluations	45	47	8
Parents' opinions	36	55	9

Teaching as a Career

Although teaching as a career has lost favor steadily during the last 15 years, the results from this year's survey indicate that the downward trend may have ended. In 1969, 75% of parents said that they would like to see one of their children enter public school teaching as a career. In 1983 only 45% said this.

In the 1984 survey, the question differed from that asked in 1969 and 1983, which dealt with "a child of yours." The question this year asked respondents first if they would like a daughter to take up teaching as a career; the same question was then asked about a son.

Fully 50% of those interviewed said that they would like a daughter of theirs to take up teaching in the public schools as a career. Slightly fewer (46%) said that they would like a son of theirs to make a career of teaching.

The question:

Would you like to have a *daughter* of yours take up teaching in the public schools as a career?

	National Totals %	No Children In School %	Public School Parents %	Nonpublic School Parents %
Yes	50	49	54	46
No	39	40	34	35
No opinion	11	11	12	19

The question:

Would you like to have a *son* of yours take up teaching in the public schools as a career?

	National Totals %	No Children In School %	Public School Parents %	Nonpublic School Parents %
Yes	46	45	51	41
No	42	43	37	40
No opinion	12	12	12	19

	Daughter		Son	
NATIONAL TOTALS	1984 %	1981 %	1984 %	1981 %
Yes	50	46	46	43
No	39	44	42	47
Don't know	11	10	12	10

Prayer in the Public Schools

Prayer in the public schools is an issue that has been hotly debated in recent years. A majority of those interviewed in this year's survey favor a Constitutional amendment that would allow school prayer. However, the least support for such an amendment is found among the best-educated citizens and among the youngest adult age group — and these two groups will play the greatest role in determining future trends in public attitudes.

The question:

Have you heard or read about a proposed Amendment to the U.S. Constitution that would allow prayer in the public schools?

	National Totals %	No Children In School %	Public School Parents %	Nonpublic School Parents %
Yes	93	93	95	93
No	6	7	4	7
Not sure	1	*	1	–

*Less than one-half of 1%.

The question:

Do you favor or oppose this proposed Amendment?

Those Aware of Amendment	National Totals %	No Children In School %	Public School Parents %	Nonpublic School Parents %
Favor	69	68	73	68
Oppose	24	25	21	21
Don't know	7	7	6	11

The question:

How strongly do you favor/oppose this Amendment — very strongly, fairly strongly, or not at all strongly?

Those Who Favor the Amendment	National Totals %
Very strongly	61
Fairly strongly	34
Not at all strongly	5
Can't say	*

Those Who Oppose the Amendment	National Totals %
Very strongly	49
Fairly strongly	38
Not at all strongly	12
Can't say	1

*Less than one-half of 1%.

Nongraded Schools

The idea that a student should be allowed to progress through the school system at his or her own speed and without regard to grade level wins majority support, though acceptance of this plan by the public is less than in earlier surveys.

The nongraded concept is more popular with better-educated citizens, with younger citizens, and with parents of children in nonpublic schools. It is most popular in the large cities and least popular in the small communities of the U.S.

The question:

Should a student be able to progress through the school system at his own speed and without regard to the usual grade level? This would mean that he might study seventh-grade math, but only fifth-grade English. Would you favor or oppose such a plan in the local schools?

	National Totals %	No Children In School %	Public School Parents %	Nonpublic School Parents %
Favor	54	51	58	63
Oppose	39	40	36	33
No opinion	7	9	6	4

NATIONAL TOTALS	1984 %	1980 %	1975 %	1972 %
Favor	54	62	64	71
Oppose	39	30	28	22
No opinion	7	8	8	7

Course Credit for Community Service

Widespread approval is found for a proposal to award course credit to high school juniors and seniors for community service, such as working in a hospital or recreation center, beautifying parks, or helping law enforcement officers.

This proposal was first included in this survey series in 1978. At that time, 87% said that they would like such a plan to be adopted in their own community. In this year's survey, 79% approve of this plan. However, the approval rating among parents of children now attending the public schools remains about the same (86%) as in the earlier survey.

Every group in the population gives a high approval rating to this proposal, which was strongly endorsed in Ernest Boyer's 1983 report, *High School*, an important study by the Carnegie Foundation for the Advancement of Teaching.

The question:

A plan has been suggested to enable all juniors and seniors in high school to perform some kind of community service for course credit — such as working in a hospital or recreation center, beautifying parks, or helping law enforcement officers. Would you like to have such a plan adopted in this community, or not?

	National Totals %	No Children In School %	Public School Parents %	Nonpublic School Parents %
Yes, would like plan	79	77	86	78
No, would not	16	17	12	16
No opinion	5	6	2	6

NATIONAL TOTALS	1984 %	1978 %
Yes, would like plan	79	87
No, would not	16	8
No opinion	5	5

PERENNIAL ISSUES

Major Problems Confronting the Public Schools in 1984

Although discipline continues to be cited most frequently by respondents as the top problem with which their local schools must contend, parents who now have children enrolled in the public schools mention this problem significantly less often than in 1983.

In the 1983 survey, 29% of the parents interviewed named "discipline" as the biggest problem of their schools; 23% mentioned discipline in this year's survey. Since parents of children now in school are likely to be best informed about discipline, their views must be given special credence.

The top five problems found in the 1983 study are also the top five problems cited in 1984. Next to discipline, "use of drugs" and "poor curriculum/standards" are mentioned most often. Tied for fourth place are "lack of proper financial support" and "difficulty getting good teachers."

The question:

What do you think are the biggest problems with which the *public* schools in this community must deal?

	National Totals %	No Children In School %	Public School Parents %	Nonpublic School Parents %
Lack of discipline	27	28	23	36
Use of drugs	18	18	20	10
Poor curriculum/poor standards	15	16	14	18
Lack of proper financial support	14	12	17	13
Difficulty getting good teachers	14	13	15	13
Integration/busing	6	7	3	4
Teachers' lack of interest	5	4	6	7
Parents' lack of interest	5	5	6	7
Low teacher salaries	4	3	6	5
Pupils' lack of interest/truancy	4	4	4	4

(Continued on next page)

Drinking/alcoholism	4	3	5	5
Large schools/overcrowding	4	3	4	8
Lack of respect for teachers/other students	3	3	4	2
Problems with administration	3	3	2	4
Crime/vandalism	3	3	2	2
Mismanagement of funds	2	1	2	5
Lack of proper facilities	2	2	1	1
Moral standards	1	1	2	2
Teachers' strikes	1	1	1	2
Communication problems	1	1	2	1
Parental involvement with school activities	1	*	1	1
Lack of needed teachers	1	1	1	-
Fighting	1	*	2	-
Government interference	1	1	1	1
There are no problems	1	1	2	1
Miscellaneous	4	4	5	7
Don't know/no answer	10	12	4	5

(Figures add to more than 100% because of multiple answers.)
*Less than one-half of 1%.

The Public's Perceptions About Discipline

One way to measure attitudes regarding discipline is to ask respondents how serious a problem discipline is in their schools. Not surprisingly, those most closely connected with schools — the parents of students — hold different views from non-parents about discipline and about many other problems with which the local schools must deal. Thus 29% of parents with children enrolled in the public schools say that the discipline problem is "very serious." In answer to the same question, 36% of those who have no children in the public schools say that the discipline problem is "very serious."

The question:

How serious a problem would you say discipline is in the public schools in this community — very serious, fairly serious, not too serious, or not at all serious?

	National Totals %	No Children In School %	Public School Parents %	Nonpublic School Parents %
Very serious	34	36	29	32
Fairly serious	34	34	35	38
Not too serious	22	18	29	25
Not at all serious	4	3	6	3
No opinion	6	9	1	2

One of the perennial problems facing the public schools concerns public relations. The media are prone to limit their coverage of news of the schools to what journalists describe as "spot" news — happenings or events that take place in the schools. Unfortunately, these stories usually concern vandalism, drugs, absenteeism, theft of school property, attacks on teachers, and the like. "Good news" is difficult to find and to report.

Consequently, the public receives a distorted picture of schools and tends to regard them as blackboard jungles. Evidence of this comes from a question that asked respondents to estimate how often certain disciplinary problems occur in their local schools.

Analysis reveals that the perception of schools as blackboard jungles is likely to result from an exaggerated idea of the specific disciplinary problems that occur in a school system; this is certainly true when the perceptions of the public are compared with those of teachers, who are most likely to know the actual situation.

For example, as many of half of the respondents in this year's survey feel that drugs are used in their local schools "most of the time" or "fairly often." Similarly, about one-third of the public feel that theft of money or personal property, drinking of alcoholic beverages, theft of school property, and carrying of knives or other weapons occur "most of the time" or "fairly often."

The question:

As I read off the following problems by letter, would you tell me how often you think each problem occurs in the public schools in this community — just your impression?

NATIONAL TOTALS	Most of the Time or Fairly Often %	Not Very Often or Almost Never/ Never %	Don't Know %
Schoolwork and homework assignments not completed	64	23	13
Behavior that disrupts class	60	29	11
Skipping classes	56	31	13
Talking back to/disobeying teachers	56	32	12
Truancy/being absent from school	53	36	11
Use of drugs at school	53	33	14
Selling of drugs at school	47	37	16
Sloppy or inappropriate dress	47	42	11
Cheating on tests	46	38	16
Vandalizing of school property	39	49	12
Stealing money or personal property belonging to other students, teachers, or staff	38	46	16
Drinking alcoholic beverages at school	35	50	15
Theft of school property	34	51	15
Carrying of knives, firearms, or other weapons at school	29	55	16
Sexual activity at school	24	57	19
Racial fights between whites, blacks, Hispanics, or other minorities	22	64	14
Taking money or property by force, using weapons or threats	18	66	16
Physical attacks on teachers or staff	15	71	14

The Goals of Education

The goals of education are difficult to separate from the goals of life. It is equally difficult to separate the responsibility of the schools for reaching these goals from that of other institutions in American life.

Nevertheless, this year's survey attempted to obtain some evidence of how the public rates the importance of many suggested goals. The ratings given to the goals listed reveal a pragmatic people who view education primarily as a means to economic success rather than to intellectual development. Near the bottom of the list is the goal of appreciation of the arts and letters, learning as a lifetime program, and participation in the democratic process.

The goals are listed below on the basis of the number of respondents who gave a "10" (the highest rating) to the goal in question.

The question:

I am going to read a list of possible goals of education. I would like you to rate the importance of each goal on a scale of zero to 10. A zero means a goal is not at all important and should not be part of the public school program. A 10 means a goal is the most important goal — before all others. A rating between zero and 10 means you consider the goal to be somewhere in between in importance.

Highest Rating

	National Totals %	No Children In School %	Public School Parents %	Nonpublic School Parents %
To develop the ability to speak and write correctly	68	65	74	71
To develop standards of what is "right" and "wrong"	64	63	68	61
To develop an understanding about different kinds of jobs and careers, including their requirements and rewards	56	54	60	54
To develop skills needed to get jobs for those not planning to go to college	54	52	59	61
To develop the ability to use mathematics for everyday problems	54	52	56	60
To encourage respect for law and order, for obeying the rules of society	52	52	54	53
To help students make realistic plans for what they will do after high school graduation	52	50	56	43
To develop the ability to live in a complex and changing world	51	50	57	42
To develop the desire to excel	51	49	56	51
To develop the ability to think — creatively, objectively, analytically	51	49	55	58
To help develop good work habits, the ability to organize one's thoughts, the ability to concentrate	48	46	52	42
To prepare for college those who plan to attend college	46	43	53	57
To develop the ability to deal with adult responsibilities and problems, i.e., sex, marriage, parenting, personal finances, alcohol and drug abuse	46	44	49	43
To gain an understanding of science and technology	45	43	50	51
To help students get good/high-paying jobs	45	43	51	43
To help students overcome personal problems	45	42	51	45
To develop the ability to understand and use computers	43	41	47	51
To develop the ability to get along with different kinds of people	42	42	43	40
To gain knowledge about the world of today and yesterday (history, geography, civics)	42	40	46	39
To encourage the desire to continue learning throughout one's life	41	40	45	39
To develop respect for and understanding of other races, religions, nations, and cultures	39	39	39	39
To develop an appreciation for and participation in the arts, music, literature, theater, etc.	35	33	39	37
To develop an understanding of democracy and to promote participation in the political process	33	32	35	32
To develop an appreciation of the "good" things in life	32	33	32	24
To promote physical development through sports programs	20	19	23	19

Who Should Determine the Curriculum?

If the public were given the right to decide who should have the greatest influence in deciding what is taught in the public schools, the top choices would be the local school board and parents; the public would give the state government and the federal government relatively little say in this matter.

This view is in sharp contrast to the policies followed in most nations, where the national government typically sets the curriculum.

The question:

In your opinion, who should have the *greatest* influence in deciding what is taught in the public schools here — the federal government, the state government, the local school board, local public school teachers, or parents of public school children?

	National Totals %	No Children In School %	Public School Parents %	Nonpublic School Parents %
Local school board	27	29	25	29
Parents	24	22	30	23
State government	17	18	14	16
Teachers	11	11	11	12
Federal government	9	9	9	4
Don't know	12	11	11	16